CASEWORK EVANGELISM

Casework Evangelism

STUDIES IN THE ART OF
CHRISTIAN PERSONAL WORK

By
CHARLES REED ZAHNISER, PH.D.
*Executive Secretary, Pittsburgh Council
of the Churches of Christ*

With Introduction by
CHARLES M. SHELDON, D.D.
Author of "In His Steps"

NEW YORK   CHICAGO
Fleming H. Revell Company
LONDON AND EDINBURGH

New York: 158 Fifth Avenue
Chicago: 851 Cass Street
London: 21 Paternoster Square
Edinburgh: 99 George Street

INTRODUCTION

I HAVE been greatly attracted to this study of Dr. Zahniser's for several reasons. His own personal knowledge of the subject takes it at once out of the region of theoretical discussion and brings it immediately into the place where the pastor or social worker finds himself facing the actual facts of human experience. And I have been greatly interested in his approach to the entire subject of practical evangelism because I have for a long time been convinced that the church worker and the social reformer need to acquaint themselves with all phases of human need, taking into account all possible factors of heredity and home surroundings and employment, and especially the conditions which go with housing and companions and religious or minus-religious training. The need of knowing all this is imperative if the minister or capable evangelist is to reach lasting results. In this careful and searching study of Dr. Zahniser's the results tabulated are removed from the field of theory and carried into the realm of actual experience. It is especially this part of the work that makes it, in my opinion, exceedingly valuable to any pastor or social worker. The cases quoted and the methods of approach in each

case cover so many different examples of human
need and of the personal contact required that,
summed up, they seem to illustrate a remarkable
scope of effort, one worthy of very careful study
on the part of those who in any capacity are trying
to find the causes for moral and spiritual lapses
and the means for lifting the human up to the
divine.

I can most heartily commend this work to ministers and all religious and social labourers in every
field of humanitarian effort. It appeals to the most
common-sense faculties and is, in the right sense
of a word that may truly be used of spiritual matters, scientific, because it is not a vague or hap-
hazard or questioning method of reaching human
need, but is based on facts that need to be taken
into account before results can be reached. Without discounting the special work of the trained
evangelist or the regular methods of the ministry in
its preaching and teaching, it brings to the aid of
these agencies plans and methods that seem to me
to be a tremendous help for accomplishing the very
things the earnest and honest reformer and pastor
wish to secure.

Dr. Zahniser brings to this work the rich experience of years of careful and trained experience.
He was a pastor for fifteen years, followed by
fourteen as Executive Secretary of the Pittsburgh
Council of Churches, and has been a recognized
leader in Protestant forces in a great metropolitan

centre. He has had rich years' experience as a social service worker in many places, including trusteeship of a state penitentiary, and membership in a great many charity, civic, and welfare organizations. For the last twenty-five years he has been in Pittsburgh, and identified with practically all its philanthropic and welfare agencies.

If pastors, teachers in Bible schools, civic clubs, welfare and evangelistic committees will study this work and be guided by its great common sense and true methods of approach to needy humanity, it will be a splendid aid to the methods that supplement and complement the work of the Church. It reveals new truths about old humanity.

CHARLES M. SHELDON.

Topeka, Kansas.

PREFACE

THE purpose of the following studies is frankly evangelistic. They start with the assumption that the gospel of Jesus Christ is the one effective panacea for all human ills and the one way into a life in every sense worth while. But they find their occasion in a conviction that the traditional evangelism is not inclusive, that there are great ranks of people and whole areas of life it has not been reaching. The reason for this is believed to be a faulty technique which it is hoped the suggestions herein may help to correct.

The program does not include methods of approach to the ordinary constituency of the Church, for which it is believed there are already at hand pretty well established ways of procedure, particularly the method known as " Visitation Evangelism " which has been developed by Guy H. Black and A. Earl Kernahan [1] and which the proposals herein are intended to supplement. Of the four general types of prospects in evangelism, herein designated as " Lambs of the Flock," " Lost Sheep

---

[1] Cf. *Visitation Evangelism*, Kernahan (Revell), and series of pamphlets on same subject privately published by Guy H. Black, Greencastle, Indiana.

of the House of Israel," "Wandering Sheep," and "Other Sheep Not of This Fold," visitation evangelism is probably best adapted for the first and third and may be effective for the second, though in that the gospel meeting or rescue mission unquestionably is of great value. But both of them are ineffective for the fourth class and for many in the second. This is the field where casework evangelism is needed.

Nor are the proposals offered here intended to take the place of the work of social agencies outside the Church. They are rather to supplement them. There will always be need for the trained and expert professional social worker. The call for his services will be increased rather than otherwise by the development of casework evangelism on the part of the churches. But there is a distinct contribution needed by multitudes of erring and troubled souls which can hardly be expected of mere social agencies. That contribution is in the way of a spiritual dynamic for the attainment of a better life, and just such a spiritual dynamic this discussion assumes religion to be. Men need a dynamic of this nature as distinctly as they need a vision of better things and a desire for better things. "If to do well were as easy as to know what were well to do, chapels had been churches and poor men's cottages princes' palaces," but just because that is not the case, the chapels and cottages remain.

DeSchweinitz, in his excellent little work,[2] has a chapter devoted to " Dynamic " in which he sets forth out of his wide experience as a social worker, how religion affords just this when given a chance. For some reason he injects into the same chapter certain other things under the same head which are not dynamic at all, but at the most inducements or incentives. But this does not obscure the outstanding dynamic character of religion as he has seen it in operation. The whole argument of the following pages rests on a profound conviction that in religion is manifested the power of God unto salvation from everything that degrades, and that we can therefore say in all sincerity to erring, suffering souls, " Ye shall receive power after that the holy spirit is come upon you," and that it will enable them to rise out of all that trammels and corrupts.

While much that follows is in the way of suggestions drawn for church workers from the field of social service, it is not to be inferred from this that social work is in all regards superior to that of the churches. It is not. Of the two, the Church has brought vastly more of weal into human life than has the whole of social service outside of it. What is more, social workers are sometimes lacking in some of the virtues which deeper religious experience has produced in consecrated

[2] *The Art of Helping People Out of Trouble*, Chap. **XIII.**

workers in the churches; virtues such as self-sacrifice, humility, unfeigned pity, and the love that suffereth long, vaunteth not itself, seeketh not its own.

It would be the height of presumption for social workers to assume general superiority over the workers in the churches. But this should not blind us to certain values they have developed, particularly in the way of technique. These pages were not written primarily for social workers. They were written for people in distinctively Christian service, and are therefore concerned particularly with what these latter can secure for the enhancement of their own effectiveness from experiences in the social field.

The case studies given in Part Two are all actual cases, most of them having been under the personal observation of the author. They are given here with names changed and sufficient other changes to prevent identification, but with nothing modified that has bearing on the significance of the stories.

C. R. Z.

Pittsburgh, Pa.

CONTENTS

PART I

CASEWORK IN THE FIELD OF EVANGELISM

PART I

CASEWORK IN THE FIELD OF EVANGELISM

I

WHY CASEWORK EVANGELISM?

THERE is a sense in which the gospel of Jesus Christ is always the same. There is another sense in which it is always changing.

It is always the same in that the revealed love and grace of God proclaimed in it are as constant as the unchanging goodness of God Himself. It is the same in that in Jesus Christ, who said of Himself, " Before Abraham was, I am," and, " Lo, I am with you alway, even unto the end of the world," is revealed the one only Redeemer in all generations. In other words, the redemptive work of God revealed in Jesus Christ is as old as human need and will continue as long as men are mortal. More than that, the great basic needs of human souls which that gospel meets are the same always and everywhere. They are such as inhere in human ignorance, weakness and perverseness. All of us err sometimes and so need the guidance and provident care over our lives which are promised in the gospel; none of us has enough moral stamina, enough spiritual dynamic in and of himself to overcome every temptation and measure up to every responsibility. There is something of a twist in the nature of every man which sometimes asserts itself in unwillingness to choose the path known to be right; so that there is always need of help from a " Power other than ourselves in the world that makes for righteousness," on which one may draw for his spiritual invigoration. In all such regards the gospel is ever the same, and one is justified in saying that the old-time religion, good enough for father, is good enough for me.

But it does not at all follow that the method by which that gospel should be presented is always the same, nor even that this is true of the form of the message itself. On the other hand, both of them need to be changing constantly because of the changes in human affairs. Men are not always the same. They are always different, different in their situations, their conditions, their outlook, their felt needs, their yearnings.

Because of this, in the first place, the message itself should be different at different times and places. This does not mean a perversion of the gospel, it means only wise selection from it. It is the Christian's boast that his gospel is as big as any possible human need, that in Christ was re- vealed " all the fulness of the Godhead embodied, and in him ye are made full." But just because this is true, the gospel's fulness transcends what any man can comprehend or appropriate. None of us can take in all of it, but all of us are privileged to take therefrom according to our needs. It is therefore important that the gospel be presented to every man in terms of the needs of his own life and, to that end, that the worker know something of what those needs are.

Jesus likened the wise worker in the things of the kingdom to a wise householder, in that he brings forth out of his treasury, the gospel, just the challenges and assurances that apply to the life of the person he is trying to win. Happy also is the preacher whose messages are thus adapted to his times; adapted in the sense that they interpret the needs of those times in terms of the gospel and they bring forth out of the gospel just that which meets the needs disclosed. He is the true prophet. Like David, he is one who succeeds in serving his own generation according to the will of God.[1]

From the same reason the method of presenting the gospel should be adapted to the changing situations and outlook of men.

Evangelism is propaganda. As such, it undertakes to influence human conduct, and it is to be presumed that it will therefore be subject to the same principles that govern all other endeavours of similar nature; and accordingly the form of its presentation will have to be different at different times and in confronting different conditions. This is true of such other projects as commercial adver-

---

[1] Acts 13:36.

tising, political campaigning or educational projects. All of these are constantly changing in
forms and methods. No business man would think
for a minute of depending today on the advertising
methods of a generation ago. If he did, he would
soon be out of business. Nor does the politician
try to win in these times by the type of campaign
that was effective in the days of " Tippecanoe and
Tyler, too." In all such matters men take it for
granted that forms and methods will have to be
changed constantly to meet changed conditions
and situations.

Now, evangelism is not only like them in that
it, too, undertakes to persuade men and to influence
their conduct, but, what is more, it undertakes to
do so to an extent far beyond any of them, for it
seeks to secure a change of the entire course of a
man's life. There is, therefore, every reason to
expect that its form, also, must change according
to the conditions of human life confronting it.

Yet, as a matter of fact, many Christian people
fail to realize just this, and as a result suffer un-
called for anxiety and discouragement. Some
earnest but indiscriminating souls, when they see
some evangelistic method of former times no longer
effective, begin to wonder whether the old gospel
has lost its power or the modern Church its candle-
stick. Sometimes also the same sort of thinking
leads to criticism of new evangelistic methods, as
though, forsooth, those proposing them were throw-

ing discredit on the religion of their fathers. None
of these would occur if these people only realized
that the same psychological principles apply to
evangelism which have occasioned much greater
changes and readjustments on the part of the other
enterprises mentioned—and that, too, without
causing anxiety among those promoting them.

WHY VARIETY IN FORMS

First among the factors compelling changes in
evangelism from time to time are the conditions
under which men find themselves. These determine in no small measure how they are to be ap-
proached. A half-century ago, particularly in the
rural districts and smaller communities where most
of the people then lived, it was relatively easy to
get a crowd of non-professors of religion to attend
a " protracted meeting." They went largely because there was no place else to go. It afforded
them an opportunity for diversion and social fellowship. Today, with so many interests crowding
in on one and clamouring for his time, there is little appeal in merely providing some place to go;
most of us are embarrassed already by having so
many such places to go that we have difficulty
deciding which to select. As a result, few people go to religious meetings nowadays except for
a religious purpose. You have to get a man
about three-fourths converted before he will attend church at all. Some forty years ago, a

cynical wag scribbled on the pillar of a small town church:

> *"Some come here to show fine clothes;*
> *Some come here to meet fine beaux;*
> *Some come here to sleep and nod—*
> *And a very few to worship God!"*

That was probably about forty times as true then as it is now. The seaside boardwalk and many other places offer so much better opportunities to show fine clothes, and there are so many more attractive places also to meet fine beaux or to sleep and nod, that folks not seeking to worship God usually go elsewhere. This means that evangelism nowadays will have to be done mostly outside of meetings.

In those former times, also, when most of the people of America lived in rural districts and small communities, they had most of their contacts with neighbours who lived round about them, which easily made for sustaining one more contact with them in the neighbourhood church. But today life everywhere is becoming urban. This is true even of the small communities. Urban, that is, in the sense that one's different contacts are with many different people, often widely scattered. Instead of listening to music where the village blacksmith plays the drum and the grocer the violin, while the doctor or 'squire leads the choir, we " tune in " on Boston or Schenectady or Chicago. Instead of going to visit neighbouring uncles or other relatives on Sunday afternoon, we motor for a weekend to some popular resort. As a result, there is much less of the intimacy of neighbourliness which formerly opened doors for the evangelism our fathers found effective.

Along with these have gone also changes in the character and time of our employment, families no longer generally working together on their own projects, but scattered about working for salary or wages among other people. Profusion of literature, new types of recreation, radical changes in home life, many factors such as these inhering in the conditions under which people find themselves living, affect profoundly all their responses and compel constant changes in the programs of all enterprises that seek to influence their conduct. Evangelism need not expect to be an exception.

Another factor, and one which grows in part out of the one just discussed, is to be found in the felt needs of men. Some of these, of course, are constant and reappear in every man's life. But this is not true of all of them. Some that were outstanding in former times are no longer felt, others appear that are new. For example, civil freedom figured largely in New Testament times, when the majority of men were slaves, but in America today freedom in a very broad sense is taken for granted. In the same way, escape from the drunkard's craving for strong drink, so much in evidence in recent years, will probably figure little in one or two generations hence, when the saloon will be only a terrible tradition.

On the other hand, the tremendous drive of our modern strenuous life, already speeded so high and still being accelerated more and more, is presenting new needs, new anxieties. The temptations of solitude have been supplanted by those of the crowd, the needs of man combating with nature by those of man with man. The increase of solidarity and interdependence requires a large development of the ethics of the team. Young women taken out of the seclusion of the home into public industry feel needs of different kinds from those of the pioneers' daughters.

One's appreciation of the gospel is always in terms of his own needs which he believes it will satisfy. To the abused and hopeless slave or the bed-ridden sufferer, the assurance of a life beyond the grave means more than it does to the free young American just starting on a promising life career. To the drunkard salvation means, first of all, freedom from the domination of an evil appetite; to the anxious parent, divine help to rear one's children aright; to the socially-minded, direction and assistance from God in making one's life worth while in the world. Our evangelism, to be effective, must in every case so present the gospel in terms of this person's felt needs as to convince him of its worth for his own life. It will be different where the felt needs are different, it will change as they change.

Still another factor which affects the evangelistic program in a somewhat different way, but just as profoundly, is the new knowledge succeeding generations obtain. A significant parallel in this regard is to be seen in education. Pedagogical policies and programs, ideals and technique have undergone changes in the opening years of this century perhaps as far-reaching as those following on the work of Pestalozzi. No one would think today of promoting an educational system that ignored the findings of modern psychology, or the relation of nutrition to mental development. Now, the aims and endeavours of evangelism are just as directly involved and profoundly affected by the newer knowledge today available in several fields.

Take, for example, matters of psychology. Freudianism may be more or less of a fad, but that there are suppressed impulses and resultant complexes which profoundly affect character and conduct and must be taken into account in trying to help people make proper adjustments, probably no informed person will question. Arrested development with certain quite clearly defined characteristics of persons of any given mental grade, and certain pretty definitely established processes to be followed in dealing with each of them, are now so generally accepted and followed in educational work and other lines of endeavour, that it seems

unnecessary to more than mention the importance
of the same being done in evangelism. No educa-
tor or social worker forgets in working with a low-
grade moron, for example, that this type must be
influenced almost entirely by suggestion, and we
should realize we will have to proceed in much the
same way in evangelism.

Hence it is that church forces need today to give
particular attention to the technique of casework
in social service. The main outlines of this technique have now become standardized, and a volum-
inous literature has grown up in recent years in
which it is set forth. The experience embodied in
this literature is rich in suggestion for those who
would make use of the gospel of Christ for human
betterment.

The need for this is the more in evidence because of the modern emphasis on the doctrine of
the kingdom. If we are thinking of this world as
a wilderness of woe that is not our home and of
ourselves as commissioned to keep crying, " Save
yourselves from this untoward generation," we will
make one kind of program of service. But if we
are thinking that " God sent not his Son into the
world to condemn the world, but that the world
through him might be saved," if we are thinking
of ourselves as called of God to fellowship with
His Son in establishing here on earth the kingdom
of God, if we are thinking of the values of the
Gospel we urge upon others in terms first of all of

how it will enrich their lives here on earth and make their daily living in every way more worth while, then we will proceed in a very different way. We will formulate our interpretation of the gospel in terms of the needs of lives as we see them. We will seek for those approaches to people in which we can best arrest attention and interest, through knowing their situations and the yearnings of their hearts. We will try also to follow up their cases till we see the assured fruition of the implanted divine unction in lives permanently established on higher levels.

It is considerations such as these that are now calling for a recasting of programs of personal Christian service in terms of modern scientific knowledge and procedures. We, as Christian workers, want the best technique of personal service for the help of fellow-men that modern scientific social service has developed, but we want to use it in bringing to bear upon needy souls the spiritual dynamic assured unto us by Him who said: " Ye shall receive power after that the Holy Ghost has come upon you." And we want the fruitage of the new life in Christ to be seen in the very betterments of human life for which the social worker yearns and strives, ofttimes with a keen sense of impotency. A combination of the evangelist's dynamic and the social worker's skill; that is the outstanding need.

Something of this combination is what is sought

after in this series of studies. Their purpose is, on the one hand, to point out to the inexperienced Christian worker how he can make his personal work for others more effective by understanding the principles of the social worker's art and developing skill in it; and, on the other hand, to train and develop in each church a number of additional workers for the assistance of the pastor in evangelistic social service, particularly among those classes of people hitherto largely unreached by the ordinary work of the churches.

II

SOCIAL AND EVANGELISTIC CASEWORK

WHAT is known as scientific casework had its beginning in the field of medicine, where the casework method has long been in use. As a method of study it is inductive rather than deductive; that is, it starts from the particular, the concrete, and ascertains therefrom the general and abstract. The method is applied to treatment as well as to diagnosis. A careful study is made of each particular case to ascertain all the facts bearing on it in any way and of the effect of everything done in the course of treatment, both on the case as a whole and on any particular factor in it. From large numbers of such cases, carefully studied and classified, have been built up the theories of modern medical practice. And the process still goes on.

This is an important part of the program. Every new case is studied, both to determine its proper classification and treatment according to the theories established on former cases, and for any new facts that may bear on the theories. No reputable physician of today would think of undertaking treatment of a case in any other way.

Nor would his patients knowingly permit it. In medical practice casework is now universally recognized.

In more recent years the method has been introduced into a number of other fields, such as the study and practice of law. Law schools now generally put their students to work studying actual cases, so that they may learn therefrom the principles of law involved and the correct practice in relation to them. Law practice is now also carried on in much the same way. Likewise, in pedagogy casework has come into common use. The same is true in practically all of the psychological sciences.

But it is in social service that casework has come into most prominent use. So much is this true, indeed, that the term is often used in this connection alone. Its introduction into this field, which began some twenty-five years ago, has been all but revolutionary. Today it is practically dominating the field. The older type social, or rather welfare, workers, usually came into the service with no special training. Goodness of heart, honesty, and ability to carry on the routine of their tasks were pretty much the only requirements. As a consequence there were many blunders, and abuses of many kinds developed, largely the result of workers' unfitness because of lack of training and ignorance of proper approach. Efforts to relieve poverty often resulted in pauperizing those helped, so that their last state was worse than their first. Delinquents grouped together as such in one " criminal class," and so treated, generally became worse under the treatment. Causes of troubles, unless of a very patent kind, were usually not dealt with because not known, usually not even sought after. Social service was largely a process of treatment akin to the administering of headache powders; it tried to remove symptoms rather than to delve back after causes.

Then, in the closing decades of the last century, came the rise of the science of sociology, and along with it the introduction of a scientific approach to the study of cases of people in trouble. A technique of social diagnosis comparable to that the physician uses with physical ills has now grown up, whereby to study these cases and to ascertain both the exact nature and the ultimate causes of them. Alongside of it has come also a technique of treatment in which the policies established like those in medicine have to do primarily with causes and with trying to remove them. Or, if this has been found to be impossible, with undertaking relief in ways determined largely by these ascertained causes. This is what is known as social casework at the present time.

CASEWORK DEFINED

Social casework may be defined as: *A program of service to individuals or families, based on*

*scientific principles and undertaking to help them
out of their troubles and into wholesome living.*[1]

First of all, it has to do only with individuals and
families. It is not concerned except incidentally
with civic, political or other social programs. The
relationships of the family to individual interests
are so intimate, however, that experience has shown
they will usually have to be considered together.
The great majority of child welfare and boy problem cases, for example, are found to be primarily
family problems. That is, the home went wrong,
and as a result the child went wrong also. Indeed,
so frequently are family interests found to be in
the fore in casework that it is sometimes spoken
of as a program of family service. That, however,
is an unwarranted restriction of the term, as there
are many cases in which family relationships are
not particularly involved.

In the next place, social casework is outstandingly a program of service. Everything in it is
undertaken with this end in view. It is frankly a
practical science, concerned always with what to
do, thus differing from investigations undertaken
just for the knowledge to be obtained. It is true
that out of the experiences of workers in this field
has come a large part of the material on which the

---

[1] It seems rather remarkable that so few efforts at definition of casework are found in the literature on the subject.
Even Miss Richmond in her classic *Social Diagnosis* simply
proceeds to use the term in relation to her presentation of
cases, but nowhere defines it.

sociologist builds his science and formulates his theories, but to the social worker this use of his discoveries is merely incidental. He studies the case of the pilfering boy or the broken home that has come into his hands with just one object in view; that is, to learn how these people and others like them can be helped out of their troubles and into wholesome living.

Much of the foregoing might perhaps be said of the old-time welfare worker or Christian philanthropist. That which is distinctive of social casework is that it proceeds on scientific principles. It begins with diagnosis. It undertakes precisely the kind of patient, exhaustive study of everything bearing on the case in hand that is followed in medical work. Particularly does it concern itself with causal factors, in the hope that these may be removed and thereby the resultant troubles will permanently right themselves. Quite commonly these are found to be remote from the trouble first noted, as will be seen in various instances of mental complexes to be studied later.

Different instances of troubles of the same kind will often be found to result from widely different causes, just as one may have a headache from any one of a score of physical ailments. It is a well known fact that no two persons are precisely alike in every way, but it seems we have been remarkably slow in realizing that because of this there will be no two cases of trouble to be treated in just

the same way. Diagnosis must therefore always
be careful and exhaustive. So far-reaching is the
importance of this study of the causal factors in
every case that Miss Richmond entitles her classic
treatment of the subject into which she put the
carefully analysed results of her wide experience
Social Diagnosis, the implication of the title itself
being that diagnosis is the nub of the whole science.
And such it is. We are always so much nearer the
solution of any problem when we understand just
what it is, that ordinarily the course of treatment
is relatively evident when diagnosis has been carefully and exhaustively made.

This means that the scientific case worker never
comes to any case with a set formula with which
he expects to meet its needs. Still more, he does
not expect ever to obtain any formula that will fit
all cases. He knows no such formula is possible.
He is at the farthest pole from the nostrum vendor
who offers one bottle of mysterious concoction to
cure everything from chilblains to tuberculosis.
He studies every case with a realization that it
will present a little different combination of elements from that presented by any other case, and
so will require a little different kind of treatment.
Accordingly, he prepares to map out his course of
helpful service anew for every person he tries
to help.

In this regard casework differs from a certain
type of so-called " personal work " in Christian

service that has sometimes brought discredit on church work generally. Personal work in Christian service may be defined as *all efforts by individuals with individuals to win them to Christ and to Christian living.* But quite commonly the term has come to connote an unstudied and sometimes intrusive procedure on the part of earnest but rather temperamental people who have tried to meet the needs of all sorts of cases by one and the same rather meagre program. They urge people to " Come to Jesus," and stress the assurance that " Whosoever shall call upon the name of the Lord shall be saved," both of which they interpret in terms of a rather narrow emotional experience. They find an easy explanation of the many cases in which they fail by saying that these are people who have failed fully to " believe," " repent " or " surrender."

DISTINCTIVE FEATURES OF CASEWORK
EVANGELISM

Casework evangelism undertakes to combine the values of social casework and personal evangelism. From the one it takes a method, from the other a dynamic. It proposes to proceed according to the best scientific technique of special casework, but depending for success on the divine power available through our Saviour Jesus Christ. It differs from personal work of the type just mentioned in a number of particulars such as the following:

First of all, it begins, as does social casework, with diagnosis. The whole program is built on careful study of the life to be helped. To approach a total stranger with a ready prescription for all his spiritual ills, usually couched in a few stock passages of Scripture, may sometimes be effective but usually is not and always is extremely hazardous. Casework evangelism undertakes first to develop an acquaintanceship wherein the worker shall be enabled to know the spiritual needs and the doors of approach to the prospect and to secure the confidence in himself that means so much in persuasion. In some cases this can be accomplished quickly, even in a single interview, but ordinarily it will require time, perhaps weeks or months. In every case decision is sought on issues understood, saving grace is offered for needs keenly felt, treatment waits on diagnosis.

From this it follows that, ordinarily, casework evangelism presumes a prolonged process. It looks upon its task as an extended one in which the decision for Christ sought by the traditional personal worker is one step. The case worker takes it for granted that the case he has accepted may be on his hands for weeks, even for years. He knows that the causes of the troubles with which he has to deal have been long developing, and he assumes their removal will only be by a course which will probably involve many discouragements, many stumblings. He knows as well as anyone that the

Ethiopian eunuch was converted by one conversation, but he recalls also that none of us knows what forces had long before been paving the way in the eunuch's heart or what experiences the eunuch had after he got back to Ethiopia.

Of course, there are outstanding examples of sudden conversions in which lives have been completely changed. But the fact that they are outstanding indicates they are exceptional. On the other hand, we must not blind ourselves to the other fact that there are far greater numbers of people whom this hit-and-run method of Christian work fails to win. We have absolutely no right to say that this is just because of their perversity of heart or of our own lack of faith. It is much more likely to be because of our lack of good judgment, careful study and patient perseverance.

Particularly patient perseverance. Here is a marked difference between the practice of the trained social worker and that of many representing the Church. The social worker understands that when he takes a case he is to stay with it as long as there is need; in other words, till he succeeds. It may take months, it may take years, it may be there will always be need of sympathetic support. But in any case the worker is to stay through. There is no place in the program for giving up a case and dropping it. How different often is the situation among church workers! Very commonly reports are brought in like this:

" Oh, I spoke to that man, but it's of no use! "
Even pastors have been heard to say, when evangelistic work in their parishes was being discussed and some names were mentioned: " We've
tried to get those folks before, but they are not
interested." Or, " No use going after them.
We've tried before, and it was no use! " The
case worker in Christian service believes God never
gives up a case, and neither should we. He assumes that failure can only be because of insuf-
ficient study or patience or loving tact on our part.

In the third place, casework evangelism is distinguished in that it involves the whole of life. It
rests on an interpretation of the gospel which
keeps to the fore the sufficiency of that gospel for
every human need and the concern of our heavenly
Father for all of human life. It assumes there is
nothing of human ill it is not set to remove, there is
nothing of human helpfulness it is not here to promote, there is no human soul we should not expect
to see fully redeemed. It concerns itself with the
whole of man, with all of his interests, not merely
with his attitude toward Christ and God. It real-
izes that the lives of real folks are not segmented
into sequestered compartments, but that each life
must be dealt with as a whole, in which each interest is affected by every other one. Indeed, personal acceptance of Christ may sometimes be the
very thing that should not be urged first.

Helping a man get a job or a woman adjust

domestic troubles or a child get better surroundings may be the first step and the deciding part in
the eternal salvation of any one of them. Whiting
Williams,[2] on the basis of wide experience as a
common labourer in steel plants, coal mines and
similar places, tells us that the constant prayer of
these people is " Give us this day our daily job! "
Their *bete noire* is unemployment. To be the in-
strument in God's hands of answering this prayer
of the jobless man may be the first thing to do
toward his spiritual redemption. General Booth
used to warn against trying to talk Christ to a
hungry man till after his stomach was filled.

On the other hand, casework evangelism differs
just as much from social casework. It differs in
that it frankly puts dependence on divine power
for success; and that, not in any general sense such
as one might affirm for any worthy undertaking,
but in the traditional evangelistic sense of the
transforming power of the Holy Spirit in the re-
generation of the soul which accepts Jesus Christ
as Lord and Saviour. It differs, further, in that it
is not so professional; it is put forward as a program for ordinary work-a-day folks who would live
helpfully as Christians among their fellow-men,
rather than for persons who plan to give their lives
to such work in a professional way.

Indeed, one of the criticisms that can properly

[2] *What Is on the Worker's Mind,* p. 282 *et freq.*

be made of present-day tendencies in social work is that of professionalizing it too much. Jesus taught that the Christian life is essentially a life of service, declaring that He Himself came among us as one that doth serve and that " as the Father sent me into the world, even so send I you." Never, perhaps, in Christian history has this truth been so emphasized as today. And it is well that it is so. But the best type of this service is not that by which one makes a living. It is the helpful contacts of everyday life among one's neighbours and associates. Often it is the service that one renders to a needy person by first bringing him into that circle of one's associates in which help is imparted by personal contacts.

This is not something that can or should be delegated. It is a part of one's religious life and worship which one cannot hire another to do for him. A state of society in which we might have organizations of professional workers whom we could employ to render every kind of needed human service, would be no better from a Christian standpoint than one in which we could hire men with prayer-wheels or priestly functions to do our worshipping for us in the churches.

Casework evangelism is offered as the way for bringing the richest joy into the lives of those who engage in it as well as help to those who are served. It " is twice blessed; it blesses him that gives and him that takes." The writer of the epistle to the

Hebrews said of Jesus Himself that He, " For the joy that was set before him, endured the cross, despising the shame! " He found that joy in serving men and seeing them benefitted thereby. This joyous privilege is what is offered to every one who gives himself to such service as a follower of Jesus. We do not want to pass it over to hirelings. Professionals in specific lines of social service we will always need. But we need also that intelligent, patient personal service of one to another which comes when the spirit of Christ, given free course in our hearts, may work out along sane lines scientifically discovered.

III

THE FIELD OF CASEWORK EVANGELISM

G RANTED that casework is desirable and of value in social service, why should it concern us as Christian workers, and particularly why should it do so in relation to the programs of religious agencies? This question is properly raised, and its answer will be found instructive.

UNREACHED AREAS

The most patent reason perhaps is that there are whole areas of population which the traditional program of the churches has failed to reach and which are of a type in which casework has been found effective by other agencies. These unreached areas can readily be seen by analysing the church membership of any good-sized community and setting it over against a similar analysis of the population of the entire community. It will be found that the church membership is ordinarily composed almost entirely of people from certain social groups and having certain types of antecedents. The writer heard the late Sam. Hadley say, not many years before his death, " In all my twenty-three years in Jerry McAuley Mission, I have never seen a man saved there who had not had a praying mother, a godly father or a Sunday School training in his early life! " That remark led the writer to put a test of this kind to scores of audiences of church workers involving thousands of people. The test put usually included in the enquiry whether they had Christian neighbours, Christian literature, Christian playmates and intimate associates—not necessarily all, but at least three-fourths of the conditions mentioned. In every case the response has been nearly unanimous, in many cases entirely so.

Now, on the other hand, it is a well known fact that the great majority of gangmen, habitues of low resorts, police court characters, and the like, have had few such influences surrounding their earlier lives. Around Jerry McAuley Mission, in the period mentioned by Mr. Hadley, thousands of boys and girls had grown up under the contaminating surroundings of the notorious East Side in which it was located, to furnish a large proportion of criminals and vicious characters of both sexes and moving out into all kinds of wrongdoing, but the mission had failed to reach them.

The same thing can be seen in the very geographical location of the churches. A typical industrial town of some twenty thousand population, recently studied, has a railroad running through the middle of it. Between the railroad and the river live more than half of the people, and in that territory is most of the degradation and poverty, squalour and need, flagrant vice and crime. But all the white Protestant churches are on the other side of the railroad. A survey of the downtown section of a large city showed a population of some seventy thousand, over fifty thousand of them white, more people living in the area than ever before, and yet within twenty-five years, in which the territory had gone through pronounced social changes, two-thirds of the white Protestant churches had been abandoned or moved away, and those that remained were able to account for less than one in twenty-five of the local white population in the rolls of both church and Sunday School.

Explanations of various kinds are freely offered for situations such as these, but when they are all considered the fact remains that, under the traditional type of evangelism in our Protestant churches, the boy and girl born and reared in a Christian home will in all likelihood become a Christian, and people coming from conditions of the other sort in all likelihood will not. This is not to say the gospel is not equal to the needs of these people. It is only to say that our evangelism has not been of a kind adapted to reach them. If we really mean what we say when we talk about a "gospel for every life and for all of life," there can be no question that we must proceed in some other way to reach these other groups. Not to do so would be to acknowledge defeat and to confess that here were instances of human need our gospel could not meet.

But there is no cause for such acknowledgment. Agencies that proceed by the casework method are able to reach these people. Not infrequently, as the churches have moved out from given districts because of changes in the population, social agencies doing casework have moved in. Religious agencies, also, with a distinctively religious message, but using the casework method, have been able to reach people of these classes, as witness some cases described in Begbie's *Twice Born Men*.

THE KINGDOM THEOLOGY

A second reason for introducing casework in church programs is to be found in the kingdom theology already mentioned and in the aims of evangelism it sets forth. The far reach of this is hardly yet realized by any of us. It is compelling us to recast pretty much the whole program of the Church, because if we think of the purpose of the gospel as having to do first of all with getting this world right with God, we shall of necessity proceed in very different ways from those we should follow if this were not the case. It is a social theology; cannot help but be. As such, it recognizes the fact that one's life courses are the product of the interaction of his inner impulses and his environment, and that both of them are therefore to be the subjects of the redemptive processes. Herbert Spencer defined life as " the continuous adjustment of the internal relations to the external relations." Not a very satisfactory definition of life, perhaps, but a true statement about it. And because it is true, our evangelistic concern includes both the external and the internal relations and the adjustment as well.

Putting it another way, there are two things about which we, as Christians undertaking to promote the kingdom of God are concerned: One is that there shall be better people in the world, and the other is that there shall be a better world for the people to be in. The social theology shows us that these two are dependent on each other. Neither can be attained if the other is neglected. They will have to be sought together. Moreover, the continuous problem of every one's life is one of adjustment. He is born into a world to which he must adjust himself continuously, even to live. Within a few moments of his birth he must adjust himself to breathe. He must adjust himself to subsist on different kinds of food, to protect himself against varying temperatures, to resist or escape powerful enemies without and microscopic ones within his own body. Throughout life he must adjust himself to his fellow-men in a thousand and one ways. He must adapt himself to living with them whether he wishes to or not, for they are all about him. He must adjust himself to them in ways of getting a living, in relation to their laws and customs, in matters of health, of pleasures, of property rights, of conflict of interests.

The best and most enduring service we can render to others is therefore usually in the way of promoting those adjustments that make for wholesome living. People in trouble are people who have not been able to adjust themselves. Sometimes it is to their external relations, so that they are perhaps in poverty or in conflict with the laws or breaking in health; sometimes it is to their internal relations, so that they are in mental conflicts, are emotionally unstable, are the prey of impulses and passions; sometimes it is to both. All of these concern us. For the gospel of Jesus Christ affords both a way of life and a spiritual dynamic to walk in it, so that the Christian worker can come to his cases with confidence that every one who accepts it can find therein that wherewith he can effectively make the adjustments he needs and come into a life of joy and peace.

But to find the particular succour in the gospel which will be effective in making just the adjustments needed in any particular life is by no means a simple problem. This is what calls for a casework program on the part of the Christian worker. One of a naïve unthinking faith may leave it all to God, urging only a simple " surrender," and then in case of failure attribute the failure to lack of faith, or afford himself some other " alibi." But

the case worker will find in one failure only a
challenge to study the case again, start a new
course of treatment and try, try again, till enduring success is obtained. Not that case workers
always succeed. They do not. Their experiences
are replete with failures, some of which are later
overcome, some followed by others again and again.
But their percentage of ultimate successes is far
greater, and their program has no place for giving
up anyone as beyond help of some kind.

From all this it follows that a third reason for
church workers being schooled in casework and
practicing it, is the variety of human situations
and needs. The very fact that different persons
are given to the same sinful practices, from very
different causes, some of them because of mental
subnormality or conflicts, some because of physical ailments,[1] some because of companions, environment or improper education,[2] should be
sufficient evidence that there is need of careful
study of each case and of helpful service adjusted
to what is learned about it in this study.

Thus the social gospel leads into courses of treatment in every way individualistic. It has little to
say about " the sinner," much to say about " this
sinful man," " that erring girl." Just as in crimi-

---

[1] Healy gives numerous instances of pilfering, habitual
lying, etc., which corrected themselves following treatment
for physical defects. Cf. *The Individual Delinquent, freq.*

[2] Certain gipsy tribes are said to teach their children it is
a virtue to steal. Cf. also John 16: 2.

nology we no longer talk about " the criminal," but about this offender and that offender, and as we proceed in a similar way in practically all the other social and psychological sciences, so here we must learn to proceed from the facts of individual lives, not from general assumptions about classes of people.

The modern theologian tells us that our theology should, first, come out of life; second, interpret life; third, return into life.[3] This means for us in this connection, first, that what we may expect to know about any sinner we will learn from studying the life and situation of this particular sinful person; second, that we will try to interpret what we thus learn in the light of the Scriptures and of the experiences of others, and, third, that we will do all this for the one purpose of helping this particular sinner into a wholesome adjustment of his own life.

RELATION TO SOCIAL AGENCIES

Just how far the field of casework undertaken by church agencies will extend cannot yet be determined. However, it will certainly not be found covering all that now occupied by other social agencies. Rather, they will supplement and support it. We shall still need associated charities, child welfare agencies, hospitals, and similar in-

---

[3] J. H. Snowden, Art. in *Western Seminary Bulletin*, Vol. V, No. 5.

stitutions, entirely apart from the Church. We shall still need the expert social worker for his special tasks in all kinds of social betterment work. Probably the churches as such will have even less to do in the way of affording institutional care. That at least has been the whole trend since Reformation days, and it seems to be a wholesome one. They will do little in the way of affording material relief; much will be in one form or another of personal service.

Personal service, however, is a large part of what men most need. Eighty-five per cent of the cases handled by the average charity agency are ones calling for personal service rather than for material relief. Devine found the outstanding causes of human misery to be in the maladjustments resulting from being out of health, out of work, out of friends and from the adverse conditions of dependent families.[4] Most of these are to be relieved by intelligent and sympathetic personal service. Moreover, great numbers of cases of trouble and distress in every community never are brought to the charity agencies at all, never should be. In every community there are always numerous needs for such service which are of kinds which cannot, should not, be made the subject of professional attention, but which at the same time call for the most skillful and sympathetic handling on

[4] *Misery and Its Causes,* E. T. Devine.

the part of friend or neighbour inspired by the spirit of Jesus. Among these may be mentioned incipient cases which if neglected will lead to more serious troubles requiring official interference or institutional care. Follow-up cases of persons released from such oversight constitute another large number to be handled in this way. Foreigners and other unadjusted groups in the community afford still more.

The proposal for casework on the part of church agencies is therefore in no sense that the churches take over the work of other social agencies. It is rather that they shall equip themselves to do effectively the work in their own parishes which is now fumbled over or not done at all. Social workers have often complained that the churches failed with cases turned over to them because their workers did not know the technique of scientific casework. The reply is, Learn the technique!

IV

DIAGNOSIS IN CASEWORK EVANGELISM

C ASEWORK literature ordinarily uses the terminology of medicine, in which the method had its rise, and the terms of which seem well fitted to its purposes. Like medical practice, social casework covers a scope which falls naturally into the following analysis:

Diagnosis, or the study of evidence; undertakes to answer the question, What is the trouble and what caused it?

Prognosis; undertakes to answer the question, What will happen in this case if left alone or if under treatment?

Therapeutics, or treatment; is concerned with the question, What shall be done about it?

Prophylaxis; turns attention also to others and raises the question, What will prevent such cases?

The same analysis will be found to apply to personal Christian service, although not always so manifestly so. Evangelism includes a great deal of service among people of thoroughly normal experiences and so, as we shall see when we come to consider the program for such work among one's ordinary neighbours, diagnosis particularly will not be as much in evidence there. But with the more difficult cases which evangelism of the ordinary kind fails to reach, and with which these studies are particularly concerned, the need of diagnosis is unquestionable. Such cases call for careful and prolonged study.

The real trouble with any one's life and the real causes of the trouble are almost never displayed readily to others. All of us wear more or less of a mask by which we try to conceal them from our fellow-men. We do it perhaps as a matter of pride or of shame, perhaps to prevent knowledge of it interfering with some of our purposes, perhaps as a mere matter of etiquette. But all of us do it.[1] What is more, we seldom know ourselves just what is the matter with ourselves. Oliver Wendell Holmes found John's opinion of John to be very different from John himself. People ordinarily attribute their troubles and particularly their sinful practices to entirely different causes from the ones actually back of them; and they generally are honest in doing so. It is even harder to get John's opinion of John to conform to the real John than that it is to get other people's opinion of John to do so. Very few of us can successfully diagnose our own cases. Yet without correct diagnosis the gospel has small chance to do its perfect work with any of us.

---

[1] Cf. De Schweinitz, *The Art of Helping Out of Trouble,* Chap. 1.

FOUR MAJOR CLASSES

To start with, there are four general types of persons to be reached with the gospel message:

1. First of all are what may be called "the lambs of the flock," children trained in Christian homes and Sunday Schools, whom we try to lead in the tenderness and relative innocency of childhood to accept Jesus as their Saviour and Lord and to devote their lives to Christian ideals and purposes.[2]

2. Then there are certain older people who may be called "Lost sheep of the house of Israel." That is, they are people who were reared under wholesome Christian influences and taught considerable of the truths of the gospel, but have drifted away from their early training into careless or selfish lives or perhaps have fallen low in sinful practices.

3. A third class, which may be designated as "Other sheep not of this fold," is to be carefully distinguished from the one last mentioned. Frequently this is not done, and the confusion occasioned thereby probably accounts for much of our failure to reach these people with our messages. This class consists of people who have never been privileged to receive Christian training of the kind we give the children under our care. Because of this they are without the background possessed by

---

[2] The program of service for children will not be further considered in this study.

the people of the second class which was just discussed and against which we are able to throw our
appeals effectively. Appeals to memories of
Mother's prayers and early Christian teachings
which may melt to tears a renegade from a good
home are meaningless to one who never knew
either. In this third class are most of the foreigners and their children, also persons reared in the
slums, gangsters, habitual criminals, and characters in general who are the products of places like
New York's East Side whom the Jerry McAuley
Mission so signally failed to reach, though situated
right among them.

4. There is still a fourth class that should be
mentioned, though they are frequently not thought
of as objects of evangelism. Continuing to use
scriptural terms, they may be designated as " Wandering sheep " of the flock. They are members of
the Church who have never become active in Christian service and who have now drifted away into
indifference. Many of them have moved their
households, but not their church homes, and now
have no active Church membership anywhere.
People of this class are usually products of a type
of evangelism which sees conversion as an end
rather than a beginning. Their acceptance of
Christ was little more than an acknowledgment of
His lordship and probably a decision to give up
certain cherished sins. It was made with an extremely narrow conception of the Christian life,

which conception has never been enlarged by careful follow-up.

Now, the mere enumeration of these classes should be sufficient to show that entirely different programs will be necessary in trying to reach each of them, and that it is of vital importance that diagnosis go at least far enough to ascertain to which of these classes each person one is trying to win belongs. When we shall get to the questions involved in programs of treatment, we shall see that a type of message that would be effective with a man of the second class might be meaningless with one of the third class and could easily be tragic with a child of the first.

THE INDIVIDUAL CASE

But diagnosis must go farther than this. It must go into the personal situation of each individual far enough to discover the real causes of his sinful practices or of his failure to avail himself of his higher privileges in Christ. This is not to say that it should be an intrusive inquisitiveness. Of course the Christian worker is to be always a gentleman, never prying from mere curiosity, never seeking secrets of others to be made the subject of idle gossip. But there will be no such discourtesy when the worker is conscientiously, consecratedly, sympathetically and humbly trying to lead another into the joys of the fellowship of Christ. He will seek only that information which will be of help in pointing the way. But he will seek this persistently and tirelessly.

SOURCES OF EVIDENCE

Social and spiritual diagnosis, as already stated, like that in medicine, is concerned with the things which determine the nature and constitute the causes of trouble and misconduct. Its constant question is, What is the trouble, and what caused it? This requires a constant search for and study of evidence and is therefore concerned, first, with securing evidence and, second, with weighing it. These two should now be considered in order.

Taking up the sources of evidence, let us consider a typical case. Here is a girl picked up by the police and brought into the Morals Court. Where shall the important facts about the case be secured?

1. The subject herself is the first source. There is the information she intentionally gives about herself, and there is also that she unintentionally or even unconsciously gives, which is often much more significant; her appearance, her actions, many things to be gathered from studying the person herself are significant.

2. A second source is her family, usually the most fertile source next to the subject herself. This includes not only what other members of the family say about the person being studied, but the observations the worker may be able to make on

the family itself. Conditions in the home generally throw a flood of light on the conduct of those living in it. Eighty-five per cent of several thousand boy cases once studied by a Y. M. C. A. secretary doing work among juvenile delinquents were found to be family problems. That is, the home had gone wrong and therefore the boy had gone wrong. Experienced social workers practically always enquire immediately into the family relations in seeking to understand any case they are investigating.

3. The community from which the subject comes is another. The character and tone of community life reflect themselves in every person in the community. There are subtle influences in its social atmosphere that do this. Usually they do so by influencing us to conform. In some cases they stir one to rebellion against them. In either case they profoundly affect character and conduct. The moral standards, the social norms, the ideals and sanctions of the community in which any one dwells are important considerations in learning the pertinent facts about his or her course of conduct.

4. The school is another source; the character of the school itself, and the record the subjects made in it. Interviews with former teachers are frequently of great value.

5. The doctor of the family is often consulted by social workers with valuable results. The intimacies which a good family physician usually enjoys enable him to know facts that he can bring to

the assistance of the case worker, and that without betraying in any way the confidence of his patient which he properly keeps sacred.

6. Other sources are her employer, neighbours, associates and perhaps the local clearing house of the social agencies, some of which may have had informative experiences with her before.

Not all of these mentioned will be consulted in every case, and still others will in some cases be found helpful. The important thing is that the case worker quietly but persistently undertake to find out all possible information and then carefully weigh every bit that is secured in connection with every other significant item. Personal history is secured as far as it may appear to be of significance for the problem in hand.

INTERPRETATION

Turning now to the interpretation of information, two things will be sought: First, the detection of misrepresentation, and, second, the elimination of error. These may, and frequently will, involve securing expert counsel. Evidences of mental subnormality or aberration will perhaps call for the help of psychoanalyst or psychiatrist. Others may lead one to bring into consultation some specialist from charity organization, juvenile court, or other social agency.

Prognosis and prophylaxis, while not parts of diagnosis, are ordinarily of help in determining the proper course of treatment. What will happen to this girl if she is left alone? What will prevent other girls from getting into the trouble in which this girl finds herself? Facing these questions will often throw further light on what to do to be of help to the case in hand and furnish new zest in the effort to do so.

Diagnosis as thus built up in the experience of careful and skilful social workers seems simple. But it is not always as simple as it seems. It takes time, much time, patience, sympathy. It involves a very different program from that of the so-called personal worker of the proverbial type, who ignores entirely such information as is above suggested, and who presses for and expects immediate conversions as the product solely of earnest solicitation and prayer. Now, the technique of casework approach does not mean the ignoring or minimizing one whit of the importance of earnestness, humility and prayer. Indeed, it implies more of them, as continued study reveals more needs on the part of the soul for whose salvation one strives.

It means following more fully the exhortation of Paul to become " a workman not to be ashamed, rightly dividing the word of truth." For the Greek word in that text which is translated " rightly dividing," and which is taken from the ceremonial of the altar of sacrifice, means " rightly applying each part." As the officiating priest was to place each part of the sacrifice and of the accompanying material in just the right position on the altar, so the skilled workman in soul-winning will be the one able to apply just the proper Christian assurance to each point of need. But to do this calls for a knowledge of the needs of each particular life and the avenues of its approach as well as the gospel assurances, and this is the aim of spiritual diagnosis.

V

PSYCHOLOGY AND SIN

CASEWORK in medicine and social service has always made extensive use of psychology. Medical practice considers the mental states of its patients to be of concern to it not only because they are often the result of physical conditions, but also because they are so commonly causes of physical conditions. Neuroses causes psychoses, but psychoses just as truly cause physical disorders, particularly functional ones, so that the physician with this in mind includes investigation of the mental condition of the patient as a regular part of his diagnosis. He would not think of blocking out a course of treatment without taking it into consideration. The same practice prevails in scientific social work. Charity and child welfare agencies constantly make use of psychological study of their clients, as do those also who deal with delinquents in courts or penal institutions. In all these the course of service is adapted to the mental factors discovered, and is often governed in large part by them.

In religious work we have been entirely too slow to appreciate the importance of this. Generally we have ignored psychological factors entirely. Such psychology as has figured at all has been of the introspective type of former generations. We have divided people roughly into two classes: those who were morally irresponsible because mentally defective or insane, and those who were normal. Those in the first class we then proceeded to ignore in our evangelism, and those in the second class we proceeded to treat all in the same way. The folly, not to say the tragedy of this, is too evident to need any extended discussion.

Whatever excuse there was for this neglect in the past does not obtain now. Very great progress has been made in psychological research in recent years, particularly in applied psychology, which is rich in suggestion for work along religious lines and which we cannot afford longer to neglect. Early in the present century the work of Binet and Simon, two French scientists specializing in child psychology, resulted in a practical set of tests for mental measurements which have since been elaborated and corrected by other scientists and are now in wide use in social and educational work. About the same time general attention was attracted to the work of certain Austrian scientists, Sigmund Freud, Jung, and others associated with them, who built up what is known as the theory of *psychoanalysis*. While much in this theory is today the subject of dispute, there is no question that their work has produced a large amount of well demonstrated and significant material which is of immediate value to social and religious workers.

In the meanwhile, building somewhat on the work of these men, but working out also along lines of their own research, certain American scientists, notably Dr. William Healy, have made wide investigations among delinquents, particularly juvenile offenders, which have produced a mass of material and established principles which are of far-reaching significance and value in this connection. Still later has come *behaviourism,* as yet too new for its values to be determined, but doubtless destined to contribute some valuable suggestions, particularly in the way of programs for influencing conduct; and that, too, entirely apart from the rather crass materialistic philosophy of some of its present outstanding exponents.

All of these schools of thought have real contributions to make to us. Aside from controverted questions, there is a large amount of material in the discoveries of each of them about which there can scarcely be any controversy, and which is of immediate and important significance for programs of religious endeavour.

ARRESTED DEVELOPMENT

Outstanding among these is the theory of arrested development. This may be stated briefly as follows:

1. Mental qualities and powers develop gradually and according to a fixed scale; perceptions, memory, association, apperception (forming concepts), judgment, etc. In the average normal life the mind comes to what is called maturity in the middle teen age.

2. Development may stop at any given stage. The mind of a child may develop to what would be the normal stage of a person, say, nine years old, and then stop. Such a person may grow up physically, but mentally will remain a child of nine years. The causes of this are still largely unknown. Some of them are certainly matters of inheritance. Prenatal experiences probably figure also.

3. Such arrested development is permanent and incurable. Any program for such lives will necessarily be one of adaptation to this condition, not of attempting to cure it.

Following are the main outlines of the scale as set up by Binet and Simon, and the terminology as arranged by them. This terminology is used with some variations in the extensive literature now available on the subject, but for our purposes it will be sufficient to follow the original arrangement, which is as follows:

1. Idiots; corresponds to infancy (cannot talk).

2. Imbeciles; development of child 2-6 years. These are commonly called the " feeble minded,"

and are divided into three classes—low grade, middle grade and high grade.

3. Morons; development of child 7-14 years. These, too, are divided into three classes as follows—low grade, 7-9; middle grade, 10-11; and high grade, 12-14 years.

4. Mature.[1]

Presumably moral accountability and certainly moral capability are dependent on the stage to which one has developed as indicated by this scale. The same is true of the program to be pursued in their treatment. Idiots and imbeciles will never be capable of directing their own lives, and should be provided for permanently in institutions or under other custodial care. Tests made in penal institutions frequently disclose instances of criminals, particularly persons with long records of petty offenses, whose mental rating is that of a child under seven years. It is utterly useless to try to establish such characters in self-directed upright living. They are absolutely incapable of adjusting

---

[1] E. g., Terman, in *Measurement of Intelligence,* uses the following classification:
Imbecile, mental age of 4 to 8 years;
Moron, 8 years to 11 years, 2 months;
Border line, 11 years, 2 months to 12 years, 9 months;
Dull normal, 12 years, 9 months to 14 years, 5 months;
Normal, 14 years, 5 months, to 17 years, 7 months;
Superiors, 17 years, 7 months, to 19 years, 2 months;
Very superiors, over 19 years, 2 months.
In most present-day literature on the subject the term " Moron " is used loosely for those whose mentality will not register much over 11 years, and " Border line " for those between morons and normals.

their own lives. They should always be supervised and directed by others, and will not be further considered in these studies.

The greatest problem is with the morons of the various grades, of which there are great numbers. Army tests made during the Great War indicated that they may comprise as much as forty per cent of the entire population. Granted that this is probably too large an estimate, there still can be no question that their number runs high in the millions among the people of America today. Most of them are tolerably good citizens, many of them very good. It depends on the circumstances by which they have been surrounded. Where these have been normal and wholesome the result has been a respectable and useful life. But had circumstances been different, had these people been placed where adjustments were hard to make, temptations strong and helpful influences few, probably most of them would have led as unfortunate or disastrous careers as others of their mentality who were so placed.

As would be presumed, this is most true of the low grade moron, the one of age equivalent to a child of seven to nine years. These are almost entirely creatures of suggestion. Their perceptive powers are alert, memories good, association is readily effected, emotions seem quite normal, but apperception and particularly judgment are notably lacking. It is utterly useless to try to reason with such people. They are incapable of it. They may go through the forms of it, frequently do, but it is largely a matter of imitation or following the thought forms manifested by others. Their courses of conduct are determined by the relative strength of various suggestions. Impulses pulling in different directions determine their courses of conduct according to the relative strength of the pull of each, as determined partly by native tendencies, partly by habit, experiences and training, partly by the circumstances of the time and place. Like the fabled donkey standing midway between two hay-stacks and starving to death because it could not determine to which to turn, these people are constantly dependent on the pull of this and that suggestion to determine their courses of conduct.

From this it follows that the program in dealing with such a person will necessarily be built almost entirely on suggestion. The worker largely wastes time who tries to reason with them or to appeal to their judgment. Success will come when one is able to make the approach through suggestion. It may be in the way of example, of directed associations, of removing temptations and substituting wholesome invitations. It may, probably will, make large use of emotional appeal. But in any case it will be by suggestion that success will be secured.

The same situation obtains to a large extent with

the middle grade moron, the one of mental development equivalent to a child of ten or eleven years,
with this difference: That whereas the low grade
moron is in general absolutely subject to suggestion
the one of middle grade attainment is more capable
of resisting it. Only it must be remembered this
resistance is not a result of careful reasoning and
judgment, as is the case with a normal mature
mind, but comes from a little more intelligent response to the same kind of influences dominating
the moron of low grade.

The high grade moron, or dull normal, with intelligence parallel to that of a normal child of
twelve to fourteen years, more readily responds to
helpful suggestion, makes greater use of the forms
of judgment, shows more powers of apperception,
in other words, is more nearly normal and mature.
But at the same time there is lacking particularly
the initiative and balanced thinking of the fully
developed mind and suggestion is still largely
in control.[2]

All of this throws a veritable flood of light on a
variety of cases that have puzzled, embarrassed or
disheartened Christian workers along evangelistic
lines. Take the man who " gets religion " every
winter in the revival meetings and forgets is as soon
as the fishing season opens in the spring; or the

---

[2] Cf. Binet and Simon, *A Method of Measuring the Development of Intelligence of Children*, pp. 5 ff. Also, Healy,
The Individual Delinquent, pp. 32-34 and 52-54 and Chap. 16.

intensely religious man who sings with such earnestness and apparently complete abandon to spiritual ideals, and yet cheats the next week or indulges in profanity when sudden reverses come; or the one who responds with so much emotion to an impassioned appeal followed by a touching mother-song, and a few days later reels drunk on the street.

All of these cases take on a very different complexion when considered as probably examples of mental subnormality. One is at least not so ready to dismiss them as instances of insincerity or debased hypocrisy. One has a new patience with them, a new feeling that the gospel has not failed. What is more, one has a new vision of entirely different kinds of procedure in dealing with each one of them, one in which the program of service is built on proper mental analysis. Very different results may then be hoped for, and responses and adjustments on their part of which they are by nature incapable will not be expected.[3]

---

[3] "The moral fool, or rather the fool of feeble morality exists. He can dominate by the brightness of his cold intelligence, by his indomitable energy, by his imperturbable cold blood, but his intelligence is temporary, fragmentary, it will not allow him to see the difference between good and evil. In spite of education these notions are totally strange to him. As there are persons entirely destitute of musical feeling, for whom music is only the most disagreeable of noises, so there are beings who have never felt the impulse of goodness, whose heart has never beat with a noble idea. These are the most unendowed, no matter what enviable situation they may occupy in the world."—Dr. Paul Dubois, *The Influence of Mind on Body*, p. 8.

SUPPRESSIONS AND PERVERSIONS

In 1881 Dr. J. Breuer, a famous specialist in nervous disorders, living in Vienna, in treating a case of a young woman afflicted with a nervous disorder including hysteria, partial paralysis, disorders of speech, etc., discovered that there had been a keen disappointment in her earlier life which, however, she had herself forgotten. He suspected that this was the real cause of her present malady, and undertook an adjustment of her life in this regard. It was secured, and she recovered. This led Breuer into speculations and hypotheses which his brilliant pupil, Sigmund Freud, took up and developed into what is called the theory of psychoanalysis.

Simply stated, the theory is in substance as follows:

1. No mental experience is ever entirely obliterated. In a sense, one never forgets anything; what we assume is forgotten, entirely departed from us, has in reality only been driven or allowed to drop down below the level of consciousness and remains an active factor in the subconscious or unconscious mind. Particularly is this true of suppressed impulses or desires, such as those we refuse to gratify because we consider them sinful or harmful and those we are disappointed in not being permitted to gratify because of lack of opportunity.

2. Suppressed impulses and other mental experiences submerged into the unconscious may there

form combinations together resulting in what is called a " complex." This may even take on forms that suggest a dual personality. It frequently breaks out in behaviour which the conscious mind in no way connects with the suppressed impulses involved.

3. All human impulses root back historically into the two elemental ones of alimentation and sex. Out of the former come all the acquisitive, including much of the combative; out of the latter come all the contributive, including the moral, the sacrificial and the religious. Thus, most that is noble and beautiful in human motivation and behaviour, as well as much that is degrading and base, has its rootage in sex.

4. Complexes can frequently be discovered and analysed by expert observers through manifestations made in behaviour, through study of the personal history of the subject and through self-revelations, particularly in dreams. Freud lays great stress on significance of dreams, because he contends that in them the ordinary inhibitions of consciously directed mental processes are lifted and the subconscious interplay of suppressed impulses and desires and resultant complexes are made manifest.

Association is supposed to have much to do with the formation of complexes, particularly those resulting in misconduct, such as pathological stealing by children and adolescents. Healy gives a num-

ber of cases in which a boy or girl given to stealing is shown to have had earlier experiences in
which a sex experience involving more or less of
shock and followed by energetic suppression was
associated in the child's mind with theft, usually
by the other person involved. He proceeded to
treat these cases on an assumption that a suppressed sex impulse was breaking out in theft. In
so doing he succeeded in securing correction, thus
indicating that his assumption had been correct.[4]

Since elimination of a desire or impulse is impossible, sheer suppression is contended to be dan-
gerous. It is like damming up a flowing stream
which, forbidden to follow the course first pro-
jected, will inevitably break out somewhere else.
It may, and frequently does, do so in marked misconduct including crime. The proper procedure
is said to be not to suppress but to redirect into
some wholesome, probably some entirely different,
channel of expression.

Manifestly any such interpretation as the foregoing profoundly affects counsels of repression in
the interests of ethical conduct and spiritual purity
which have been quite common in religious circles.
It condemns wholesale asceticism and all its works.
The " crucifixion of the flesh," according to this,
naturally and inevitably brought on the lurid

---

[4] Cf. Healy, *Mental Conflict and Misconduct,* Case 9, pp.
154 *ff., et freq.* For cases of psychopathic lying caused by
sex experiences, Cf. *Individual Delinquent,* Cases 165-168 *ff.*

imagery and other unsought thoughts and impulses which distressed certain noted saints and which they attributed to the devil. Also the orgies and unnatural vices that sometimes developed among devotees in monastic institutions were but a natural reaction on the part of weaker personalities against a thoroughly unnatural manner of life. The same idea is set forth in the crude but keen analysis of a turbulent boy which describes him as like a steam engine that " must either go or blow or bust." According to this, the way to keep that boyish energy from " busting " out in misconduct is to afford it some wholesome activity in which it can " go " off usefully or " blow " off harmlessly. This counsel would expunge entirely all our categories of " dont's," unless we can couple each with an alternative " do." Every vice thus becomes a perverted virtue, and the moralist's first task in each case is to find the particular wholesome and beautiful expression into which may be directed the energies now breaking out disastrously in misconduct.[5]

Nevertheless, we must not lose sight of the fact that sin still remains sin. Such psychological ex-

---

[5] It is possible for the energy manifested by the repressed emotions to be " sublimated into legitimate channels. For instance, the sex instinct may be safely directed into philanthropic effort, religious service, intensified business or professional activity, chivalry, recreation, etc. But if it is impossible to sublimate it, the psychic energy of the repressed complex may escape the censor." Stutsman, *Curing the Criminal*, p. 242.

planations of the courses of conduct do not fully
account for them, do not reduce wilfulness and
perversity of heart to mere reactions against adverse stimuli, do not render one whit less the need
of a divine transforming power for the salvation
of the sinner. There is a something more which is
active in human behaviour than just attitudes and
tendencies of human organisms giving direction to
reactions against stimuli from without. When all
these have been taken into account, there still
remains an important residuum, a very positive
something which reacts and which in Christian par-
lance we have called " the sinful heart."

Just as there is something more to a sonata than
the relative vibrations of differently sized wires
within the piano, so there is something active in
human behaviour of vastly more importance than
the innate tendencies and external stimuli involved.
The self can no more be eliminated from human
behaviour than can Rachmaninoff and the musical
poem in his soul from that which thrills us from
the piano under his inspired touch. Despite the
naïve assumptions of some dilletante present-day
psychologists, personality is still much more than
a fetish, the soul much more than a myth. We
still need the counsel of the seer of old, " Keep thy
heart with all diligence, for out of it are the issues
of life."

Every person of much experience in the affairs
of real life knows that there are many cases of

marked misconduct which rise out of what is manifestly just " pure cursedness." There are men who know they are doing wrong, who do not blame heredity or environment or the inefficiency of the Church or anything else, who deliberately pursue their evil courses well knowing that they are evil, just because they want to do so. So marked are some such cases as to suggest that there should possibly be added a fifth group to the four-fold analysis herein made of the types of persons to be reached by our evangelism.

But a more careful observation shows that this is not the case. This perversity of spirit is not a characteristic of a distinct group. It is, rather, a taint that runs through them all and only comes out in more lurid colours in characters of this type. In some others it can be discovered in a more despicable form as it undertakes to conceal itself by hiding under pretexts of being controlled by innate or environmental factors. In every case in some form or other and to varying degree, the taint will be found.

And so these psychological findings are of profound import and fertile in suggestions to the Christian worker in the way of giving direction and form to his own program in trying to help each sinner into saving fellowship with the redeeming God revealed in Jesus Christ and thereby out of their misconduct and into a life really worth while.

VI

PSYCHOLOGY AND SALVATION

SOME years ago a revival meeting was being conducted in a rural district of one of our central states which was attended night after night by a man manifestly very much in earnest. It was a meeting in which the Methodist altar type of service was being used, and each night he responded, going to the altar, doing everything that was suggested to him, and then went away at the end of the meeting, shaking his head, manifestly disappointed. People who knew him said he had done similarly in revival meetings of all sorts for miles around during many years. This was the last such meeting he attended. Some years later he died, a disheartened man, thinking he was eternally lost.

The explanation is this: He had a favourite sister, a most beautiful Christian character, who had died. To him she was the embodiment of religion in its very best. He idolized her memory. Now, it seems she was fond of telling of a remarkable experience she had enjoyed in connection with her conversion, in which she seemed to have a vision of a burning bush like unto that of Moses, and out

77

of that she had come into the spiritual peace to which she attributed her ensuing beautiful life. This man assumed that the vision had been the important thing and that he could never become such a Christian as his sister had been until he, too, should see a burning bush. He sought it in vain, and died in despair.

The incident is given here because it is only an extreme form of a common error in which people presume that certain emotional experiences such as this are essential to securing real spiritual results. They take little or no account of diverse psychological conditions and elements or of the sequence of certain psychological processes, which determine in large measure the reactions of different individuals to gospel appeals. It is therefore well that some attention be given to these considerations here, both that we may realize emotional experiences of the kind just described are entirely incidental to real and effective Christian experience, and at the same time that we may have clearly in mind what are the essential psychological experiences in the making of a Christian character.

A little careful thinking right here will not only enable us to be of help to unfortunate victims of ungrounded anxieties such as the one just described; it will also protect us against the common error of seeking and expecting spiritual reactions to stereotyped forms of gospel appeal from people as yet without the psychological background to make them possible. All this will give direction in important details to our efforts at helping others into enriching religious experience.

FUNCTION OF RELIGION

First of all, a word should be said about the function of religion itself in casework. For it is sometimes questioned whether religion should have any place in programs for helping people out of their troubles and into wholesome living. Not a few social service enterprises have been set up on the assumption that religion should be kept out of such work. Usually this has been occasioned in large part by a fear that prejudices and suspicions between those of different sects would otherwise cause embarrassment. Unquestionably there is a real problem here for social agencies, and greatest care is needed to avoid conflict or even suspicions because of this. But at the same time as much care must be taken that we do not throw out the baby with the bath by eliminating religion itself, when what we are really after is that such service of helpfulness should not be exploited for the selfish advantage of some particular religious institution or propaganda. Believers in religion cannot feel content with its elimination because of such considerations, for the reason that to them religion is the one great spiritual dynamic without which no social service can arrive at soundly helpful results.

Much lack of appreciation of the values of re-

ligion in these connections probably arises out of
muddled or distorted conceptions of the nature of
religion. To ask an objector to define what religion is will frequently be sufficient to reveal the
ground of his protest. This is not only true of one
who conceives of it as " the preaching of soporific
truths—or untruths—to keep the mob quietly at
work while we amuse ourselves."[1] It is just as true
of many persons, like a certain group of social
workers recently described by one of their number
as believing " that religion is all right, a very good
sort of thing for those interested in it, but really
has nothing to do with success in what we are undertaking." Definition is therefore important
here. It will usually show that the objection
either is to something entirely incidental to essential religious experience, or comes from never
having understood its dynamic character as conceived by its advocates.

Religion has been variously defined.[2] This variety in definition has been occasioned partly by
various experiences with it and attitudes toward it
and partly by the relationships in which it is being
discussed. In this study we are considering it as a
factor in casework and as such is properly defined
as: *The securing of spiritual help from higher
Powers by acts of worship.* This definition is
frankly that of a believer. At the same time, it is

---

[1] Ruskin; quoted by Kidd, *Social Evolution,* p. 96.
[2] Cf. Kidd *op. cit.* for list of definitions.

intended to be liberal, positive and inclusive. Let us consider it more fully:

In the first place, it affirms that religion is a source or means of real spiritual help. That help may be thought of as coming in any one or a number of different ways; partly perhaps in the form of providential adjustments in the affairs of one's life by a superior intelligence guided by love, whether this adjustment be thought of as that of the external relations or of the internal relations involved; partly perhaps by means of so-called " leadings," either through being enabled to find the spiritual significance in the events of one's own life, to see the " providential " in one's experiences, or in the form of inner convictions, the guidance of an inner light. But in any case it will include as the most important, the essential factor, the coming from without one's self of a spiritual dynamic, a moral driving power, an inner urge that will make attainment possible where one had not the strength to accomplish it alone. It is the exultant cry of Paul, " I can do all things through Christ who strengtheneth me! " [3]

In the second place, this definition affirms that this help is secured from higher Powers. For our purposes here, these Powers may be conceived of in any of a number of ways; as the One God and Father of us all, as the Trinity, or any person of it

[3] Phil. 4: 13. Literally, " *endynamites* me! "

according to traditional Christian conceptions, as Jehovah, the Ruah Elohim of the older Jewish teaching, or even as the divine beings set forth in some other religion. What is affirmed is that the source is what Matthew Arnold referred to as "That power in the world not ourselves which makes for righteousness," what Helen Kellar set forth when her teacher for the first time tried to convey to her the word God and its meaning, and Miss Kellar replied, "I have known Him these many years, but I did not know His name!"

In the third place, it affirms that this help is secured by acts of worship. These may be and are multitudinous in form. There are, however, two essentials in worship, one or both of which is at the heart of every type. These are, first, an attitude of seeking and receptivity, and, second, response. Faith figures particularly in the first. So does prayer; prayer in the sense set forth in the familiar hymn,

> "Prayer is the soul's sincere desire,
> Uttered or unexpressed;
> The burning of a hidden fire
> That kindles in the breast.

> "Prayer is the heaving of a sigh,
> The falling of a tear,
> The upward turning of an eye
> When none but God is near."

The other essential, response, is usually in some form of sacrifice or service. It includes the thank-

offering and thanksgiving, the making and keeping
of vows, self-denials, self-surrender, testimony to
fellow-men, acts of service to them in His name.
" I will tell of all thy wondrous works." " Then
will I teach transgressors thy ways, and sinners
shall be converted unto thee."   " The half of my
goods I give to the poor; and if I have wrongfully
exacted aught of any man, I restore fourfold! "

In casework very commonly the person one is
trying to help will have very hazy notions concerning religion. His opinions about it may differ
widely from those of the worker. Some of his
ideas may seem foolish to the worker. These need
not be made the subject of adjustment first, certainly should not be made the subject of dispute
or ordinarily even of discussion in the early stages
of the treatment. That which is of first importance
is the actual use, perhaps in the most elemental
way, of the privileges and opportunities religion
affords. What we are after is to help this person
find divine assistance in meeting his needs. Plenty
of time can be taken in adjusting his incorrect
theological ideas.

Case workers need always to be mindful of the
great variety of forms in which religious experience
can normally and helpfully inhere. Narrowness
on the part of the worker's outlook is sadly common here and is always harmful. It is so easy for
one to feel that the religious life of another cannot be right unless it is run in the mould of

one's own experience, that workers can quite unconsciously come to emphasize and insist on
things not really essential, and to do so to the
bewilderment and discouragement of those they
are trying to help.

William James, in his monumental work, *The
Varieties of Religious Experience*, well sets forth
how great is the variety of ways in which different
people are affected by and express their religion,
and how vastly different are their conceptions of
it; and yet all of them are sincerely held and more
or less helpful. The causes of these variations are
manifold. Some of them lie in the different dispositions of people; what the older psychologists
called the temperaments, choleric, sanguine, melan-
cholic, phlegmatic. These particularly affect the
ways in which religion is expressed in forms of
worship, the high church emphasis on the æsthetic,
the Scottish emphasis on the intellectual, the puri-
tanic on moral rigour, that in some other quarters
on the more or less violently emotional. Other
causes inhere in environment with the presence or
absence of certain forms of temptation.

In some cases, many of them indeed, difference
is determined by education and training and by
the opinions and expectations thus engendered.
Whether one was reared among people who presented conversion as necessarily of a cataclysmic
form, momentary and accompanied by certain
types of emotion, or among others whose concep-

tion of religion was of a quietistic or a sacramental type, profoundly influences not only one's expectations but his actual experiences in matters pertaining to what he considers his soul's salvation. Still another source of marked variation in religious experience is the manner of one's former life. A refined girl brought up in the cloistered seclusion of a cultured home, or a sweet child lovingly learning Christian truths at its mother's knee, is not to be expected to have an experience akin to that of a dissolute man who for years has crushed down his nobler impulses in a prolonged practice of obstinate rebellion against his early Christian training. All of these factors are of importance to the case worker, both as significant elements in diagnosis and as having direct bearing on the program of service to be undertaken.

SEQUENCE IN NORMAL RELIGIOUS EXPERIENCE

There is, however, a certain psychological sequence in religious experience in all these varied forms, which is of a good deal of importance and needs to be kept clearly in mind by the worker. Failure to recognize this sequence has commonly caused failure and disappointment. What obtains here is a natural law in psychological experience, whether with religion or something else, and, like all natural laws, it cannot be ignored without one's getting into trouble. Moreover, this law is just the outworking in Christian experience of that principle which Jesus phrased, " First the grain, then the ear, then the full corn in the ear."

In the psychological process of the making of a Christian character there are the following four parts or stages: First, a period of seed-sowing. Second, a period of gestation or incubation—in psychological terms, of subconscious mentation. Third, an emotional crisis, commonly called conversion. Fourth, an ensuing period of development. All of these are essential; none of them can be omitted or seriously abridged without loss. And they must come in this order.

The first of these is self-explaining. In the normal experience of persons from Christian homes, it begins in early childhood and works on through ensuing years till there is a tolerably clear and full understanding of the meaning of the Christian message and appeal. With others it must be provided otherwise. Foreign missionaries are careful to work at this sufficiently long, keeping enquirers in some kind of a catechumenate, till the missionaries are confident their profession of acceptance of Christ is with something like a proper and adequate understanding of what its meaning should be in their lives. Unfortunately, some Christian workers among people in the homelands, not appreciating the value of an adequate background in this regard, have not always been so wise.

The second is just as important, but too often is not properly appreciated. Sometimes it is ignored entirely, and in such cases always with disappointment as a result. There is a well-known psychological law to the effect that information newly introduced into the mind does not at once find its place as an integral part of the mental content and attitude. If it is sufficiently different from ideas previously holding sway, it may eventually break up the old equilibrium, stir up more or less of turmoil and force a readjustment that may involve the discarding of some opinions previously held and greatly modifying others. On the other hand, it may itself be more or less modified or may be classified as false in the process. But in any case all this involves a period, usually somewhat prolonged, a large part of which is not conscious and intentional but goes on in the form of what psychologists call subconscious mentation.

There is no need of extended discussion of the character of this kind of mental process here. It is a fact of familiar experience in other regards, as in the sudden recalling of a name or word for which one has sought vainly shortly before and then suddenly it flashed into the mind, or such as is experienced in awakening from sleep with the solution of a problem suggesting itself and quickly worked out, over which one had been puzzling without success just before retiring.

Now, processes of a similar nature, but more involved, frequently go on for long periods, even for years, profoundly affecting one's whole outlook on life and attitude toward great spiritual realities and the religious appeal. The change is not usually a conscious one. It may manifest itself gradually, or it may do so suddenly. In the latter case these seems to be a sudden conversion coming as the result of influences just then brought to bear. In reality these influences were only the spark that touched off an explosion of what had been accumulating in a sort of subterranean way for a long time. Had it not been for this accumulation, the spark would have caused little disturbance.

Under the third, reference is made to what is commonly called " conversion," the outstanding desideratum of religious work. Definition, analysis and description of this form from the theological side are common in theological literature. For our purposes here we are interested only in its psychological aspects. Just what is the psychological experience of a soul undergoing what we call conversion? Perhaps the most informing answer that has been made to this is the one of William James: " The process, gradual or sudden, by which a self hitherto divided and consciously inferior and unhappy becomes unified and consciously right, superior and happy." [4]

Enlarging a little on this, and recasting it somewhat in terms of present-day psychological discussion, a definition may be formulated somewhat

---

[4] *Varieties of Religious Experience*, p. 189.

as follows: *As a phychological experience, the New Birth or Conversion consists of a revolution of the inner life, whereby accumulated subconscious processes of readjustment break through and overthrow the previous system of values and motives, and substitute a new and different system.*[5]

The nature of the fourth, which we have called a period of development, is manifest. In this, through an ensuing period of years, the new adjustments are strengthened and increased, the conception of the Christian life is constantly enlarged and growth in the Christian graces is the normal process. But these are all enlargements on the changed centre determined at conversion and are dependent on it.

COROLLARIES OF THIS SEQUENCE

Out of this sequence there follow a number of corollaries which are significant in the way of furnishing guidance in Christian casework.

Of first importance among them is the fact that the first and the second of the steps or stages above listed must both precede the third, something which is often overlooked or ignored by a type of personal workers who manifest more enthusiasm than knowledge. But familiar examples of successful personal appeal easily demonstrate it. Take, for

---

[5] This definition does not concern itself with the theological aspects of the question. Whatever may be the work of the Holy Spirit presumably takes place in the processes named. Only the results are evident above the level of consciousness.

instance, the case of Naaman's servant. He wisely waited after his master had been counselled by Elisha, until Naaman's wrath had been given time to cool somewhat and until a realization of his present situation along with his original purpose in the journey had been given opportunity to bear upon his feeling of humiliation at the hands of the prophet. Only then did he come with his suggestion that they go down to the Jordan and try it out anyhow.

Or, take the case of the Prodigal; he " came to himself," apparently without help from any one. But he did so only after a long series of varied experiences and when the accumulated impressions of them all—his early good training and wholesome surroundings, his subsequent dissipations and resultant losses and sufferings, and finally his abject situation among the swine—had merged together into an entirely different outlook on life and its values. Out of all this his decision easily came.

Moses had to have many years in the wilderness before he could see the burning bush.

Now, the same law holds in our own times. Here is a case of a faithful minister who worked for years with a man in whom he had come to take a special interest, but apparently without results. Then he left the parish, another minister came, and a couple of years later the man gave himself to Christ, apparently almost of his own accord. What really happened was that these years were a period of subconscious mentation in which the impressions made by the faithful minister of former times quietly worked themselves into the man's system of values, broke up the old relationships among them, brought about their rearrangement around different foci, and thereby produced a new outlook on life as a result of which it required little in the way of a new stimulus to lead the man to the decision that meant his conversion. But only the patient work of the first minister, followed by the period of mentation, mostly subconscious, made this possible.

A second corollary is that the character of the third, or conversion, experience will vary according to differences in the first and second. James finds a great general division of people can be made into two classes, which he designates the " healthy minded " and " sick souls." Under the healthy minded he groups all those who have enjoyed normal and wholesome religious privileges to which they have responded one by one as they came, so that the result has been a gradual and more or less constant growth in the Christian graces. In this process frequently the subject is unable to designate any one time when he was converted. Hence James says in his definition that the process may be either " gradual or sudden." Sick souls are those in which this process has been interrupted, perhaps stopped at an early stage, perhaps broken into by years of rebelliousness or dissipation, or by some shocking sorrow, disappointment or disillusionment, or perhaps there has been little or no real seed-sowing at all. In some of these cases there has developed a decided complex hostile to religion which must be circumvented or broken up before conversion is possible.

In both of these two major groups, the healthy minded and sick souls, James finds there are varieties without number, dependent on personal temperament, types of experience and training, in some cases on hereditary factors. This variation bears particularly on the emotional counterpart of conversion and is important in that connection. Had this fact been understood, it would have averted the soul tragedy described in the case described in the opening of this chapter.

Indeed, the emotional experience one may have in conversion is quite commonly different from what was anticipated or even desired. The writer recalls a case of a man and wife in a midwestern state who had been living decidedly irreligious lives for some years and who would readily be classed under what James calls " sick souls." Both of them were converted in a revival meeting in which there was considerable emotional expression. The husband, who came first, had condemned this emotionalism and expressed a determination that if he should ever make such a decision there would be nothing of this kind about it. But his conversion was marked by more emotional outburst than any of the others. His wife was so much impressed by his experience that she followed him in likewise devoting her life to Christ, and said to a friend that her one desire was for just such an experience as her husband had enjoyed. But in her case conversion came as quietly as a spring breeze.

A third corollary is that the time of the emotional crisis, or conversion, cannot be arbitrarily fixed in advance. In terms of Christian faith and hope, it might be stated in this way: One is justified in feeling assured that the friend for whom he labours and prays will some time be saved, but he cannot at all say just when or how. What has been set forth above shows at once how this must be. The instruction given, the impress of examples set, the power of persistent prayer may have no evident effect, but the effect is none the less there, stored up in the subconscious mind, where it is doing its quiet work and whence it may be expected some time to break through in some form or other of surrender to Christ. Herein lies the basis of the Christian assurance that " My word shall not return unto me void."

A fourth corollary is that, in casework, conversion should not be prematurely sought or urged. Wise gardeners do not keep digging up the seed they have sown, to see whether it has sprouted. They are patient to wait for the signs of new life to appear on the surface. So here, particularly among persons of little or no religious background or teaching. To urge decisions in such cases too soon is likely to result in suspicion and antagonism or to produce a nominal decision which has little depth of meaning. The worker must first secure the confidence of the subject in himself, in his own religion and in the unselfishness of his purpose, and ordinarily persons with little background of experience with devoted Christian people are slow to give this. It is but natural they assume those approaching them are trying to get something out of them. They have abundant reason for it in manifold experiences of life. This assumption must first be removed by straightforward friendliness and service, usually extending over some time.

Here is a case of a man of strong character, now holding a position of national leadership and influence, who was won from a dissolute life and to acceptance of Christ by a minister who laid siege to his soul. That minister worked and prayed earnestly for this man, but cultivated him for a full year before he ever said a word to him about accepting Christ. The result was that the first time he did so, the man made the great decision and shortly afterwards when he made his public avowal and united with the church, he brought seven of his associates with him. " He that believeth shall not make haste."

On the other hand, this does not at all mean that pressure should never be made for such decisions. It certainly should. It is only a question of when it should occur.   Few cases will be brought to decision without more or less of it.   Delayed conversion can frequently be brought through by strong persistent urging by the right person at the right time in the right way.   Revivals and spiritual awakenings work to the same good end.   Nor does it mean that one should ever hesitate to give a word of testimony for Christ to a comparative stranger when opportunity is afforded, or even to press for a decision for Christ if he finds a background of Christian training and understanding. Unquestionably there are multiplied opportunities of this kind allowed to go by unused by Christian people for every one where they act too quickly.

What is being impressed here is that there is a psychological process which must be permitted to work itself out.   Perhaps, as with the Ethiopian eunuch, the casual meeting with a Christian worker may come at the time when there is ripeness for decision.   But ordinarily in casework there is ample opportunity to watch the development and see evidences that the time for decision has come. The conscientious, prayerful Christian worker may have full confidence God will help him so to work that he shall not err therein.

PART II

CASE STUDIES

VII

THE FOREIGNER

OUT on one of the beautiful hills of south-western Pennsylvania there stands a historic old Presbyterian church that dates back to the time of the birth of the nation. Established by the sturdy Scotch-Irish stock of those early days, it has a splendid history. For more than a century and a quarter its wholesome influence radiated throughout the community for miles around, and out of it have gone many persons of influence whose splendid lives were in no small part the product of this church. But today there is a different population round about. The farms have been sold to coal companies, who have opened extensive mines and coke plants. The old population has moved away, a new one composed almost entirely of foreign-speaking people has come. In the valley under the shadow of the old church has sprung up a town of several hundred people. Its dirty narrow streets swarm with children, Americans of tomorrow. Recent investigations showed vice and crime to be rampant, particularly illicit liquor joints in which fathers squandered their wages while their children went barefoot and hungry. But so far as reaching these people was concerned, the historic church might as well have been a thousand miles away. None of them was in it, cared for it or thought it cared for them.

The saddest thing about this picture is that it is not exceptional. A survey made of the surrounding territory, including parts of five counties, disclosed one hundred and four similar towns with a total population in excess of seventy thousand, with no church privileges whatever and almost as many more with no Protestant work among them. And all this is but typical of the situation among the foreign population generally throughout America. It is not a matter of their being Roman Catholics, and for that reason unavailable to Protestant agencies. Thousands of them are not in the Roman Catholic Church, many are hostile to it, many never have been affiliated with it. Either they will be reached by our Protestant forces or they will not be reached at all. But they have not been reached, except in small numbers. The old program of our churches failed to touch them. Hence the churches retreated and the fields were abandoned. Among these people Protestantism failed to function.

Not that the churches did not care. They did care, and many have been their efforts, large has been their expenditure of work and money in many instances to reach these people. There have been results, but in most cases these were meagre. Missions were established, street meetings were held in which " the simple gospel " was preached, but few showed interest or even understanding. Churches established among these people, to be conducted in their own foreign languages by preachers of their own tongues, did reach some of them; but the children drifted away. They did not want to be in a " foreign " church; they were " Americans." If these people were to be reached in appreciable numbers, it would have to be in a different way.

Experience, where it has been tried, indicates that this different way is casework. These are " other sheep not of this fold," and as such are without the background of teaching and association that makes for effective approach along lines of the traditional evangelism.

A good example of this better way is to be found in another church some miles removed from the one above mentioned, but similarly situated. Only in this case, when the old membership was found to be rapidly slipping away and suggestions began to be made that this church would shortly have to be abandoned, as had so many others, there was a little group that thought otherwise. They said: " There are more people in this community than there ever were before; these people need the gospel as much as any who have ever been here. Let us stay, and let our church proceed to serve them."

But how? " By our being Christian neighbours

to them." This they proceeded to do. Here was
a magnificent home of a wealthy young business
man, whose wife was a daughter of one of the old
families in the church and who loved the old community. She, too, was the possessor of considerable wealth of her own. Across the road and a
short distance from their fine residence a row of
miners' houses was erected and occupied by people
of Slavic and other foreign tongues and manners.
This young man and his wife proceeded to be neighbours to them. They treated them as they would
others in whom they had an interest and for whom
they had respect. There was nothing in the least
supercillious about their attitude. They were
manifestly superior, but they never manifested the
fact themselves. They led these people to feel
perfectly at ease with them. Their Christian interest was so simple and sincere that one of these
foreign women, for example, would feel perfectly
free, if some morning the baby was ill, or something went wrong in her cooking, to run into the
back door of her wealthy American neighbour's
house for counsel and help. They were neighbours
to each other.

In the same manner another family, that of an
elder in the church living a mile or so away, became
neighbours to eight similar miners' families located near them. Various others of the church did
the same. The pastor, one of those quiet-mannered,
approachable men who have the knack of making

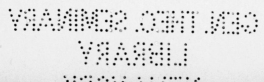

one feel at home in their presence, went about among these people constantly, made their acquaintance, put himself at their service whenever he could be of help to them, such as in sickness or in trouble. He said little to them about coming to his church; he talked about religion only when it came into the conversation in a thoroughly natural way.

What was the result? Within a few years more than half of the membership of the Sunday School in that church were children from these homes of foreigners, and nearly as large a proportion of the church attendance was from these same homes. Success came because these Christian people proceeded to act in a Christian way as neighbours to the foreigners. They taught more by their examples than by their words. They lived the superiority of their culture rather than asserted it. Then the foreigners instinctively came like the woman who said to Charles Kingsley: " Tell me the secret of your life, that I may make mine beautiful too."

Many of these people had formerly been Roman Catholics, and that in countries where the church life and ideals were far lower than here. " Does not the priest come and interfere! " the pastor was asked. His answer, so simply stated, was eloquent in meaning: " Oh, yes; there is one foreign priest who comes around and threatens them sometimes. He can stop some of them from coming to meetings, but he cannot stop us from loving them! "

There are four distinctive difficulties to be overcome in dealing with the foreigner. All of them are clearly met in the work of the church just described.

The first rises out of the foreign culture and character of these people. This is even more of a barrier than their foreign tongue. Their customs, their ideals, their moral norms, their traditions, their racial characteristics, all are different. Some of the differences are by no means inferiorities to be got away from, but most of them require adjustment, if these people are to fit comfortably into American life. And these adjustments are not easy to make. They require also a sympathetic considerateness on our part that is not always easy to attain.

A second handicap obtains in the foreign people's lack of evangelical background. Usually there has been little or no teaching in the great fundamental verities of the evangelical faith which we implant in the minds of our own children. Their ignorance of spiritual things is their greatest ignorance. As a result, our very vocabulary is often meaningless to them.

The writer was one time addressing a labour meeting where he had been invited to speak on the contribution that religion has to make to the solu-

tion of the problems of labour. In the course of
the address he emphasized somewhat the value to
the individual of the indwelling Christ, a theme of
course quite familiar to the average evangelical
audience.

After the meeting a bright, keen young Jewish
man came up and asked: " What do you mean by
the Christ? "

The young man was manifestly honest and very
much in earnest in his question. He was bewil-
dered because he did not understand our teminol-
ogy. He knew of the Christ as a name Christians
apply to a certain historical character who lived in
Palestine nearly two thousand years ago. But
what was meant by this indwelling Christ? To
him the phrase was only bewildering.

Now, precisely this is what frequently occurs in
the minds of foreigners to whom we try to bring
our messages which are framed for those who have
a background of an entirely different kind. We
forget that we cannot reap where we have not sown,
that there must have been a relatively prolonged
period of seed-sowing followed by one of gestation [1] before there is likelihood of success in seeking conversion.

A third difficulty lies in the heterogeneity of the
foreign population of this country. This means
such a variety in background and characteristics

---

[1] See above, p. 55.

that experience in dealing with one type is a poor guide for work with another. More than that, it means an intermingling among the foreigners themselves, in which too frequently it is the better things in their several traditions that are sluffed off, and a generally lowered idealism and cynicism results.

Then, fourth, there is a superciliousness on the part of Americans that is often the greatest handicap of all. A man of many years' experience in Christian work among foreigners of many types was asked: " What, in your opinion, is most needed to lead these people to Christ? " Quick as words could utter it came his reply: " Get our own people to treat them in a Christian way! "

CASE 1

John D. was under sentence of death for the murder of his wife. He was a young man of Italian parentage who had been reared in a slum district without religious training, and had been schooled from childhood in the ideals and practices of the underworld. His wife had had the same kind of background and was given to sex offenses, in which she persisted after their marriage. One evening, in a quarrel over her announced intention of going out again into the street for this purpose, both of them being under the influence of liquor, she was shot.

Following his trial and conviction, for which he

was poorly prepared because of his poverty, certain Christian people became interested and, after examining the facts in the case, felt that it was really a case of second degree murder. They therefore undertook to secure a commutation of his sentence to life imprisonment. They were unsuccessful, but the effort to secure the lighter sentence delayed his execution nearly two years.

During that time John was greatly impressed by the character and ideals of these people who were trying to help him. It all showed him a side of human life he had never known before, and he admired it, loved it. He eagerly talked with the workers about the secret of such a life, and later read with great interest the Bible presented to him. When finally the word came that the effort at commutation had failed and that he would have to die, it was a very different John who received the news. He accepted it with a resignation that showed a beautiful Christian faith, and when he went to his death it was as a man fully satisfied to accept a fate that he felt somehow a good heavenly Father would work into what is best, and as one fully assured of his fellowship with God in Christ.

But that is not all. This unselfish, disinterested effort in his behalf, on the part of Christian people, when his old companions of the underworld life had deserted him, so impressed his aged mother and brothers and sister that all of them are today members and faithful attendants of the Methodist church, the Italian associate pastor of which had been one of those active in John's behalf.

CASE 2

Joseph L. was of Croatian parentage and lived in one of the most degraded settlements of foreigners adjacent to a large industrial plant. A well-equipped and finely directed Christian Centre had been established in the community, and Joe, then fourteen, joined their troop of Boy Scouts. But he was a problem. Conceited, quarrelsome, selfish, suspicious, resentful, he caused all sorts of trouble. After some months the head worker noticed that he seemed considerably interested in certain dramatic activities that were just then being featured, and he was encouraged to take active part in them. He showed quite a little talent in this work and was soon running off helpfully in this way the energies that shortly before had been causing so much trouble.

When winter came with emphasis on athletic programs in the gymnasium Joe found interest there also. Gradually his old quarrelsomeness and petty tyrannies sloughed off, and he came to be decidedly helpful about the Centre. At sixteen he was given a position, at very modest pay, as an office assistant in the evenings. In the meantime he had entered employment in a neighbouring factory, where, after two years, he is still employed and making good progress. His evenings he still devotes to the Centre, where he does the office work mentioned, and in addition is now the assistant scoutmaster of the troop, and makes himself generally helpful about the institution, in which he takes great interest.

He has not yet joined any church. His people were of Roman Catholic antecedents, and he may some time find his church home there. But is he a Christian? One evening the head worker of the Centre and the young man who has charge of the boys' work were having one of those little heartsome talks about the work in which we all sometimes indulge, and Joe overheard them, though not noticed at the time.

The head worker had said: " I wonder sometimes whether we are really getting anywhere with these people. Do they really understand why we are doing it all? Here, I left my fine home and family in the East to put my life in here, where I really did not have to come unless I wanted to do it. I wonder whether they understand that it is all because we love Jesus Christ and want to see His power working out in their lives also? "

They chatted along in this way for a little while and then separated. The next day Joe came to her and said, " Miss A., I heard what you and L. were saying last night, and I just want to tell you that so far as I am concerned I do understand and I care. What you people have been doing and the way you have been living here with us has shown

me a kind of life I never knew anything about
before. I always thought everybody was selfish
and always trying to get something out of other
folks all the time, till I met you people and found
you just trying to do good and help folks. I
never cared anything about preaching, and I'd
go right by a 'salvation yeller' on the street
corner. I wouldn't even stop to listen. But I
see how you people live, and I want to live that
way, too."

CASE 3

The Simerick family were in desperate circumstances. Andrew and his wife already had three
children when they came from their Croatian home
to find fortune and a better life in the steel town
where Andy found employment. For some years
they got along fairly well; four more children were
born, two of whom, however, twins, died apparently because they were not able to receive proper
care.

Then came misfortune. Andy was struck by an
automobile and lay for weeks in a hospital, from
which he came out crippled for life. While he was
in the hospital some of the children were caught
stealing milk from neighbouring porches, and a
worker in a Christian institution in the neighbourhood was asked to investigate. She found the
family living in one room in a basement and absolutely destitute. The only clothing on the children

consisted of old flour-sacks that the mother had made into crude slips for them. In a squalid bed lay a six-year-old boy, hunch-backed and unable to walk. There was no food in the place; the rent had not been paid for weeks.

The first thing to do, of course, was to secure food and clothing. Then an adjustment was made of the back rent, and the family was moved out into a two-room apartment, where there would be good air, for it was already evident that tuberculosis was present. The hunch-backed boy was placed in a hospital, where for months every effort was made to restore him to health, though without success. The affliction was found to be tubercular, and from it he eventually died, yet not until after he had developed into such a sweet-spirited, beautiful character that everybody about the hospital loved him.

When the father finally got out of the hospital, influence was brought to bear at the plant where he was formerly employed, and work such as he could do was secured for him. The first money he received for this he brought to the people who had helped his family, and offered it in part payment for what had been advanced for them. Through four years the family was helped, not much in the way of finances after the first year or so, but much in the way of counsel and encouragement. The children were taken into the activities of the social work connected with the church. One of the boys made a perfect record for a year in Sunday School attendance.

In the midst of it all, Mrs. Simerick came to the Christian worker who had been helping them and, grasping her hand, in her poor broken English said: " I no know what society you belong to, but I want to join that same society."

It would be fine, in some ways, if this story could stop here. But there is more to it. And this more needs to be told, because it sets forth what so many people fail to realize, that in casework one never gets through; the case can rarely be marked off as finally closed and dismissed. The Simericks are a family that will always, probably, have to be given oversight and occasional help. They are of the type that easily gets out of adjustment one way and another—it may be with neighbours, with employment, by bad investments, by errors of many kinds, and they have to be given help in securing readjustment.

At the time this is being written one of the daughters, now in her eighteenth year, has been found to have become sexually immoral and as a result is venereally infected. She is undergoing medical treatment, and in the meantime the Christian worker interested in the family is at work trying to make out a program for her moral rehabilitation. Already she has found in her diagnosis that the girl had been led astray under the influence of a degenerate American girl, that she is very suggestible, easily influenced, has little appreciation of the seriousness either of her offenses or of her present situation. In other words, here is an entirely new case, in the same family, on which the worker will have to build a program of helpful service. Only in this instance it is not particularly a foreign problem, but akin to what might occur in the same way had her family been American.

CASE 4

The Simkivitches were Slavish. In the old country they had dreamed of the great opportunities in free America, and they had come here to educate their children and give them a chance in the wonderful country of which they had heard so much. For a time things went well in the steel town to which Mike brought his family, then came labour troubles which left them penniless and Mike practically blacklisted from a job. Like many others similarly placed, they took in boarders, ten of them, men who worked in the mills, five occupying the beds at night, the other five during the day. All these, with the family in which were now five children, were crowded into three rooms. Tuberculosis followed, which resulted in the death of Mike and left his wife in circumstances all the worse. Then the oldest daughter, now in her seventeenth year, went down with the same disease.

At this point the service of the case worker

began through a neighbour's saying to her: " Will you no go and pray with Mary next door? She about die, and priest no come to pray without ten dollar, and they have no ten dollar."

The worker of course responded, and there followed a long course of service to the needy family. The next fall the mother herself lay dying of the same disease in a hospital to which the worker had secured entrance for her. One day she said to the worker: " I pretty soon die, too. You take my children? I come this country for them. You get them education? You, you only I have now! " The worker promised.

After the mother's death there was a long struggle. For a time the home was kept together. Barbette, only fifteen, proved herself a real little mother to the younger children. At the mission, where she came constantly for help, it was really remarkable the way she could make a tasteful hat out of the lining of an old coat, or improvise respectable clothing out of other cast-off garments given her there. Mike, two years older, went to work to support the family. After six years the family is happily self-supporting, four of the five living children now working.

At fifteen Barbette confessed Christ, and wanted to join the Protestant church under which the mission she attended was conducted. But Mike objected because, said he, " I don't think mother would want her to join any other church than the

Catholic Church." As yet no final decision has been made. But the whole family continues attending the functions of the mission, and all give evidence of sincere desire to live Christian lives. Church relationships can work themselves out with time. The worker is wisely not hurrying that. But she is pushing right ahead in helping these young people so to know and live Christ that they will be of use to His kingdom and rich in His fellowship into whatever church they may finally go.

Case 5

The Husack family were Slovak Lutherans who had been in America some six years, three of them in the slum of one of our great cities, where they were found by the Inner Mission worker as a result of the oldest girl, then thirteen, having been arrested for stealing an umbrella at a department store. At the juvenile court the girl was found to have been sexually immoral also, and to be a chronic liar. She was therefore sent to an institution, and this worker was asked to look after the family. The family was found to be in abject poverty, the father having died a few years before, and the oldest son, on whose income the mother was dependent, having shortly before run away and joined the army. They were living in one room on an alley and with no income. The only other boy was a cripple, confined to bed.

The first thing done was to move the family to healthy quarters in a two-room apartment. Then work was secured for the mother, a second daughter, Sarah, helping look after the house when her mother was employed. Later Sarah secured work in a factory, and the mother was enabled to stay at home, Sarah going to night school, where she learned stenography. For eight years this family was under the care of the Inner Mission worker, all the time their condition improving as that was done, they were enabled to move from time to time to better quarters.

For the crippled boy was secured a brace, and he is now a normal healthy boy. Sarah is a stenographer in the plant where she started factory work, an active church member and Sunday School teacher. The older girl, after two years in the institution to which she was committed, came back an earnest Christian girl, has since married and is now a happy wife and mother. Recently she said to the worker who had kept in touch with her during her incarceration: " I thank God for the day I was sent there. It made a woman of me! "

A number of the foregoing cases will be seen to be cases of dependency as well as of the foreign element. They have been purposely chosen as such for the reason that such cases are so frequently found together, and in meeting the needs which dependency involves there is perhaps the most common opportunity to help foreigners into adjustment to American life.

It will be noted, too, that the result has not always been membership in the particular evangelical church under which the service was rendered, and in some cases this was not even sought. That is as it should be. There are traditional and affectional ties to the churches with which families have been connected for generations that are not to be rudely jolted or torn asunder. And, after all, what we are concerned to accomplish is personal experience of the saving power of Christ in one's own life; church membership in one's own institution is rather incidental. Our first concern is to build up Christian lives, not any institution. This is not to minimize the importance of the Church of the value of its fellowship. But it is to keep first things first.

What is more, one of the things against which we must be constantly guarded is using charity work or social service as a mere bait in proselyting propaganda. That is always deeply resented by the poor, and ought to be. The Church, as well as the individual Christian, should do good hoping for nothing in return. An admonition we all need in this connection is thus forcefully put by Dr. Karl Neumdorfer:

" Merely to subordinate social welfare-work to the missionary activities of the church . . . would obviously not fulfil the divine commandment of love. A mission would cease to be truly Christian the moment it used the plight of the poor as a lever for pushing them into a confession.

"True welfare work will be the spontaneous expression of the religious life of the church. This is clearly the way in which the early Christians understood it, as we read of them in the history of the apostles. Of course they were missionaries; but in spreading the faith they used 'words and signs,' not alms. Indeed they felt that this growth was less their own work than it was the achievement of the Lord. It was because they believed that they could not help being charitable. Their welfare work was therefore, in its disinterestedness, the perfect reflection of the spirit of Christ." [2]

---

[2] Quoted in *The Commonweal*, May, 1926.

VIII

THE ERRING GIRL

A MAN, declared Victor Hugo, may fall a hundred times and rise again, but let a woman fall once; yes, but let her look once in a wrong direction, and society brands her as a reprobate and an outcast. Grim and cynical as this appears, it is only too commonly verified in experience. Ordinarily people seem to take it for granted that the girl who goes bad will stay bad. There are many missions for fallen men, but how many for fallen women? Where are the equivalents in work for women to Jerry McAuley or Pacific Garden Missions for men? True, these institutions are open to women, and some women are redeemed there, but not many. The program attracts men, reaches men, because it is built for men. The same psychology is even more manifest in ordinary respectable middle-class community life. When a young man goes wrong, how many there are ready to help him, how much rejoicing there is when he professes repentance and conversion, how people are ready to restore him into their fellowship! But how about the girl who has gone wrong?

The simple fact is that little is done for her except of a kind that is patronizing, supercilious. We establish " rescue homes " galore, but we treat the unfortunates who have been served there in a way that makes constantly for a sense of inferiority. The scarlet letter can be burned as deeply into a soul without the use of the old-time branding iron.

It is only necessary to run through the rolls of a half-dozen average churches, counting up on one side the reformed men who were formerly guilty of crimes and outstanding breaches of decorum, and then on another side the women of similar records who are now in good standing and influence in the church, to realize that the churches simply are not reaching such women. The girl who goes wrong ordinarily finds that she has lost caste. She will get little encouragement where she has been known except of the patronizing kind. Her only hope is to go away where she is not known and start anew.

There is doubtless an explanation of this which is not far to seek. Some of it presumably comes from an instinctive self-protection on the part of others of her sex, some of it because of the discouraging difficulties that have been found because of the more disastrous disturbance the delicate and highly sensitized female seems to suffer from discovery in wrongdoing. With these we are not particularly concerned here. What is important in this connection is that we recognize the fact of her situation. From that it may be possible to move on to doing something helpful.

It should be frankly stated, also, that restoration of women who have really fallen low in habitual wrongdoing is a most discouraging business. Not only are police and reformatory records notable for the small number of restorations, but the same is true of professedly Christian institutions. The superintendent of a religious institution receiving fallen girls reported that in ten years' experience less than one in ten of the girls it had served were thereby established in wholesome living without subsequent lapses, many of them repeated lapses. Sex offenses, which of course figure most commonly, when repeated for a considerable period, seem to warp the whole moral nature and indeed the entire mental outlook, so that experienced workers are convinced restoration is ordinarily impossible without a relatively prolonged period of oversight and control which may occupy years, and even then be disappointing.

But this is not true of young and first offenders, and it is with these that the opportunity for casework on the part of church workers is usually found. Moreover, this type is by far the most numerous, and from these ranks the hardened types are constantly being recruited.

As is generally known, sex offenses far outnumber all others among women who figure in the courts. Records of the Morals Court of Pittsburgh, for example, show that fully three-fourths of the women and girls arrested by the police and brought to that court are charged with sex offenses. To these should be added many others in which, while the charge was perhaps disorderly conduct or "suspicious person," or even larceny, the offense was connected with or a result of sex irregularities. Nor is this the whole story. As already indicated, psychologists are now pretty much agreed that a very large percentage of misconduct on the part of women and girls roots back into sex. Healy has found that in relatively few out of hundreds of cases handled was the sex element not manifestly an important element. Lying, stealing, quarrelsomeness, even assaults and murders, on the part of women, on careful investigation are usually found to have their final cause in something abnormal in the sex life.

But it is equally to be remembered that out of the same source comes much that is good and noble. Nothing would be farther from the truth than to assume that sex is itself bad and only a root of evil. On the other hand, modern psychology finds in it the source of romance, the home, all the touching virtues connected with motherhood, poetry, art, religion. It is only because sex normally functioning means so much for making life beautiful and helpful and good, that its perversion means so much of tragedy. Here, outstandingly, vice is perverted virtue. The vital energies, the affectionate emotions which, uncontrolled or mis-directed, have broken out in misconduct, had they been properly controlled would have brought help-fulness and worthy joy. Correction will therefore be in the form of redirection.

Why do girls go wrong? For many reasons, of course. Wide investigation has shown that most often it is through betrayed love. Sometimes mis-led ignorance, moral weakness or low resistance, sometimes a love of adventure, the spirit of " dare." Vicious environment usually figures. Sometimes there is an abnormal high sex craving or a depraved promiscuity desire, but these are not the common sources. The desire for money—an acquisitive motive and therefore rooting back into alimentation—which becomes a dominant one with many depraved women, probably figures much less in starting girls wrong than is generally supposed. Much has been said about poverty and low wages in industry as causes that is largely surmise. True, fallen women commonly give this as a cause, but these characters are notoriously liars, particularly in accounting for their own conduct.

Careful investigation made by the writer and some associates into the life records of 506 fallen women showed that less than ten per cent had ever worked in store or office, less than ten per cent had ever worked in factory or laundry, twenty-one per cent had come directly from their homes, never having worked for wages; thirty-six per cent had come from domestic service, in which constant treatment as inferiors inevitably makes for an inferiority complex which makes a girl easy prey for the designing.

Case 6

Dora had been a problem for some time before she was brought into Morals Court. She was now seventeen, and for three years or so had been having illicit relations with the boys of the community, till she was now commonly known as a bad girl. Complaint was common about her being a very bad influence among the boys. Examination at the court showed her to be seriously diseased as a result of her immoral conduct. After considerable consultation at the court, Dora was paroled under the care of the pastor of the church where she had formerly attended Sunday School. She was given to understand by the court that if she failed to make good under this oversight she would be committed to the reformatory.

The pastor first had a long conference with Dora in his study. His approach was sympathetic, and he secured her confidence fully, so that he had little trouble getting at the real facts of the case, despite her manifest untruthfulness. Dora lived with her mother, who had been deserted by Dora's father many years before, and who did janitor work for a living. There was one brother, younger

than Dora and already a dissolute character. The
mother was well known to be sexually immoral.
Arrangements were made whereby Dora continued
to live at home, but was given employment in
domestic service in the home of a neighbouring
parishioner who was a woman skilled in social service. Dora agreed to keep in close touch with the
pastor, whom she had come to trust fully and
whom she esteemed most highly.

The investigations showed that Dora was of
fairly normal mental development, vivacious,
deeply affectionate, and responsive to kind treatment. She frankly acknowledged her sex offenses
and confessed that she had been led into them
largely because of her own strong sex craving. She
readily agreed that her course had been bad, and
seemed to come to realize during the counsels
that it must be increasingly disastrous. She readily submitted to medical treatment for the cure of
her venereal infection and agreed to stop all illicit
relations, a resolution which she kept fairly well.
In the home where she was employed she was in-
dustrious, obedient and kind.

But soon she was caught in petty thieving.
When confronted with it she denied the theft, but
brought back surreptitiously a number of things
she had purloined. None of these things she took
was of much value. The stealing was quickly
perceived to be of the psychopathic type commonly
resulting from a complex produced in such char-

acters through sex experiences and suppressions. All this was frankly explained to Dora, who seemed to understand and to want to co-operate in working out her readjustment. Her lying, another fault quite common with her, much of it mere romancing, was also taken up with her frankly, but always with the greatest kindness.

Her employer finally felt compelled to discharge Dora because of her continued stealing and lying. The pastor then secured her other employment in a place of business. As months went by, Dora improved in regard to her stealing and lying, though there were some indications that her sex offenses were occasionally repeated. However, she was evidently fighting hard to make good. It was evident also that she was doing so out of respect and appreciation for the pastor who was patiently helping her, rather than fear of the court's yet sending her to the reformatory, though that factor also unquestionably had weight.

After this course had been continued nearly two years, Dora married a young man who had been one of her former associates in her loose living. This was with the full approval and encouragement of the pastor, who was satisfied they were well adapted to each other, and that a girl of Dora's make-up would find her adjustments best accomplished in that way.

However, the case was not yet out of hand. After some years had passed and two children had been born, Dora was found to have developed a quarrelsomeness that got her into trouble with her neighbours and also with her husband. She came back to the pastor, her mentor of all these years. Her husband also came to him, though at a different time—and each came without knowing the other had done so. Again Dora was enabled to adjust herself, the troubles with the neighbours were arranged, Dora and her husband became reconciled; and now for several years there has been no further trouble.

Now, what had religion to do with all this? Much in every way. While being careful not to obtrude it, the pastor had made it plain to Dora from the first that she could not win out in her effort to come back into respectability and right living without divine help. She knew that he was constantly praying for her. Sometimes he prayed with her, though not much and always very simply, and never with any reproaches. She was fond of talking to him about the Christian teachings she had so little grasped in her limited Sunday School experience, and having him interpret them to her as they kept coming up in the light of her experiences. There was nothing artificial about this, nothing strained; just an easy, natural interjection from time to time of something about moral strength available through religion, and about the satisfying character of a life conducted according to Christian principles.

Case 7

Jeannette came out of a rather proud and respected family of some means. Her father had
got into some financial difficulties and deserted the
family in her early childhood, but the mother had
means of her own on which the family lived. At
fourteen, Jeannette was developed physically beyond her age, but mentally so retarded that she
could not make the sixth grade in school. A pri-
vate tutor was secured and worked with her for
months, but was unable to make much progress
with her. Mental tests showed her to be a low
grade moron, highly suggestible, apparently utterly
incapable of exercising judgment, moral or otherwise. Before she was sixteen the family was
shocked by discovering she had been going out se-
cretly with some disreputable boys in the community and fallen into immoral practices with them.
The fact became generally known, and the family
was greatly humiliated. What was to be done?

At this point the family pastor, who was an experienced social worker, was brought into the case
as adviser. Arrangements were first made for
Jeannette and her mother to travel for a few
months and visit friends in another city. Then
they were brought back home, to face the future.
Jeannette's situation and particularly her limitations were frankly explained to her family, and it
was made plain to them that she would always
have to be given oversight. At the same time some

capabilities she did have were as carefully pointed out. She had considerable musical talent, both vocal and instrumental. She was capable in household work which she enjoyed, and had considerable artistic taste and skill. She was fond of children and adept in pleasing them.

A program was worked out whereby Jeannette was introduced into some work in the church, helping with the children under an older and stronger worker, where she gave special attention to music and craft work. Her mother was her companion, Jeannette seldom going anywhere without her.

Fifteen years have now passed, and Jeannette has developed into a respected and useful woman. She still has the limitations that in early life got her into trouble. But wise direction, patient care and spiritual influences have enabled her to use her talent well.

CASE 8

Late one Saturday afternoon a pastor's telephone rang. It was a distracted mother calling; a widow with several children, whom he had been helping for a number of years in various ways. She had just learned that her oldest daughter, a girl of nineteen employed in a large cleaning establishment, had left work that day along with another older girl and a young man, who were going to take her to New York the next day, where she was promised an easy job with " fine clothes and lots of money."

The distracted mother, of course, knew what this would mean to her daughter, but there was little question that the girl did not.

Within an hour the pastor had given proper authorities clues by which they were able to locate the party, and the girl was arrested as a runaway and brought to Morals Court. When brought in she was highly indignant, so she was placed in a detention room till the next day. She was still rebellious, so she was placed again in confinement for another day. By that time she was ready to listen to counsel from the Christian woman court worker. Carefully, patiently, she was shown the peril from which she had been snatched. Her esteem for the pastor because of many years in which he had helped the family made her particularly ready to listen to what he had to say.

When she realized the truth about her situation she was horrified at the danger, and grateful for her escape, but so humiliated she could not think of going back to her old job. At the same time she objected strenuously to going back home. There was a reason for this which the workers well understood, so their next task was with the mother. Gently but firmly the mother was shown that she must do her part if her girl was to be saved and that home conditions and her actions and treatment of her daughter had had much to do with creating the discontent that made her an easier prey to those designing her downfall.

Then the girl was secured a new position in a large mercantile establishment in the downtown, where she would be near one of the workers interested in the case; and openings were secured into new associations with some fine young people who knew nothing of her recent experience. Close contact was kept with the home so as to be sure the conditions there which had made so much for her recklessness before should not obtain again.

Two years later she married an excellent young man she had met in these new associations; she is today an esteemed and happy wife and mother, devoted to her Lord and to the church they now attend in another suburb of the city.

Again it may be asked, what had religion to do with all this? Very much, though it cannot be seen in the mere narrative. The girl was a Christian girl, her trust in her pastor was based on his Christian counsel and fellowship through former years. Throughout the conduct of the case religion was frequently, though never obtrusively, introduced as the one great spiritual dynamic for conquest and attainment. Perhaps most effective of all was the impress made by association with the workers helping her, whom she knew to be devotedly Christian; she was therefore able to attribute to their religious experience all the fine features of their own characters which she admired and came to emulate.

IX

THE DELINQUENT BOY

BOY problems usually rise out of one of three causes: Subnormal or abnormal physical or mental development, misdirected energy, or bad environment. There are not many really bad boys. But there are very many who will become bad men if they are not helped into proper adjustments in the crucial formative years.

Casework among them is therefore pre-eminently a matter of diagnosis, though unfortunately there has been very little of it in our ordinary procedure with them. We were content with saying they were bad and ought to be punished, curbed, made to respect authority, taught their place. It is only in recent years that we have begun really to diagnose their problems, and the result has been little short of revolutionary.

The researches of such men as Dr. William Healy, who as psychiatrist in connection with the Municipal Court of Chicago has studied the cases of literally thousands of boys arrested for various offenses, and has prescribed and directed the carrying out of their treatment, have been particularly illuminating. In one group of 823 cases of recid-

ivists (repeated offenders) his diagnoses show that
in 455 cases mental subnormalities and peculiari-
tiss appeared to be the main factor in producing
the trouble, and in 135 more they figured in a less
important way.[1] In 73 there were mental conflicts
resulting from suppressions, and in 192 improper
sex experiences and habits into which they had
ignorantly allowed themselves to be led, figured as
causative factors. Abnormal physical conditions,
including excessive physical development, also figured in 273 cases, many of the cases being the same
as showed other abnormalities already mentioned.

From this it will be seen that in the majority of
these cases of children astray, there were physical
and mental conditions that needed treatment, the
adjustment of which would likely go far in helping
to correct the improper conduct. Of this same
number, 556 were found to have come from defective home conditions, including alcoholism, and 279
had been under marked influence of bad companions, thus showing the effect of bad environment.

The results secured in the course of treatment
of these cases, in which efforts were made to remove, correct or make proper adjustments to these
causative factors enumerated, are illuminating in
the way the efforts have resulted in corrected conduct. For we are justified in assuming that the
type of causes that appear here, in the more ex-

---

[1] *The Individual Delinquent*, p. 130.

treme cases requiring court action, are of a kind
with those active also among the rank and file of
other children who more or less perplex us, but
have not yet got into such serious trouble.

In view of all this the outstanding importance of
careful diagnosis in the very beginning of dealing
with any troublesome child is at once manifest.
Usually it is a case of a mentally or physically sick
child to be treated or a misguided child to be re-
directed, rather than just a bad one to be spanked.
Of course he needs the grace of God for his salvation, but the first means of grace for him may be
the doctor, the better home, the different surroundings, the wholesome outlet for energies now breaking out in misconduct.

CASE 9

Edward H., a boy of twelve years, had been arrested on the complaint of a woman for indecent
exposure on the street. The parents came to the
pastor of the church where the boy had occasionally attended Sunday School, asking him to appear
in the boy's behalf at police court the next morning. The pastor, a young man with a surprising
lack of sense of opportunity, declined to do so, and
instead sent the parents to a local politician to get
him to intercede for the boy. Now, in doing so, he
did just about the worst thing possible, particularly because he stated that he was satisfied the
boy was mentally defective and that his offense had

come because of that and not from mere badness of heart. As a result of his course the politician intervened, the boy was discharged—and no better off —and the parents found themselves under grateful obligations to the politician, who would of course collect in full at the next election, when they would feel they must vote as he might request them to do.

How much better it would have been had that pastor gone with them to the police court, explained to the magistrate why he thought the boy was defective and thereby secured a careful mental diagnosis at the hands of the city psychiatrist and started a constructive program for the boy's help. By so doing he would have done a real service to the boy and won his own way into the hearts of the whole family and probably won them for Christ and the Church. But he chose to throw away his opportunity, or rather to give it to an unscrupulous politician. The case is given here because it is only a somewhat extreme example of a practice too sadly common.

CASE 10

Harold S. was sixteen and a half years old and a great source of worry and sorrow to his devout parents. All of his troubles seemed to have developed within the past year or so. Prior to that he had been an ordinarily good boy, getting along finely in school. Now he had become lazy and listless, and, worse still, had got to stealing. He was strangely bold, taking things from stores, but more from other persons in his home. Several times he left home, shifting about for himself till his money was exhausted. Yet he was a likable fellow, and people generally became fond of him. On leaving home in the morning he would affectionately tell his mother he would " sure behave " himself this day, but before the day was over he would be again back in some wrongdoing, and in trouble.

His family made several special efforts to influence him by religion, in which they were all very devout. They took him to revival meetings, where he would respond, pray with apparent earnestness, then the next day make sport of it all and go back into his evil doing.

Harold was then taken to a psychiatrist, who made a careful study of him and, by winning his confidence, learned of certain physical troubles from which he was suffering, but which he had diligently kept to himself. These were of a character which the doctor was satisfied would soon be outgrown if he were placed under a regimen which he explained both to the boy and his parents. The result was that Harold soon ceased his stealing and other evil practices, and in the course of two years has become a fine young man.

Religion had a part, an important part, in his reconstruction. But it was religion plus, it was religion expressed in physical readjustment as well as emotional appeal.

Case 11

Johnnie R. was a rough-and-ready type of boy in his sixteenth year. He lied, gambled, fought, was irregular and unreliable in his work, playing the part of a young city tough with bravado and nonchalance. His father was dead and he lived with his mother and older sister, with whom he constantly quarrelled. In desperation the mother appealed to a man of wide experience and fine Christian character, who proceeded to make friends with Johnnie and cultivated his confidence. He soon found the real cause of the trouble.

Mother and sister, in their anxiety for his doing right, had so hemmed him about that he felt himself under constant restraint and his naturally independent spirit rebelled against it all. When his new friend talked earnestly with him about it and particularly about the future into which his conduct would certainly lead him, Johnnie burst into tears and said he would gladly stop all his evil practices if only he could get fixed somehow so that he would not have that awful feeling of restraint. On the advice of his friend, Johnnie was placed for a time in the country, where he worked on a farm and associated with Christian men. He stayed on the job for over a year. During that time he was completely changed in character, and he has caused no further trouble. What he needed as a special work of grace was a different environment till his expanding soul could adjust itself and attain self-control.

Mental conflict unquestionably figures very frequently in causing misdoings by boys, and by girls, too, for that matter. Habits of stealing, as already stated, are commonly the result of sex suppressions,[2] as are also truancy, running away from home, irritable temper, even pyromania. Secret knowledge of things which attract, but for one reason or another are not mentioned, may work out the same way. " One of our main theses concerning this whole subject is that there are substitution delinquencies. The individual gets relief, as it were, perhaps quite unconsciously, by entering into misdeed which may seem less reprehensible." [3]

Now, this which experts find to be so common among more pronounced offenders, is with all propriety to be assumed to hold in similar measure among other people as well. Which means that in every case of a reputably bad boy, there is a strong likelihood that some powerful emotions hidden from others and probably hidden also from himself, are finding an outlet in his misconduct. Ordinary church workers may not be able to analyse his complexes. They do not need to do so; but they will get much farther in their efforts to help him into wholesome living by bearing in mind that

---

[2] Cf. Healy, *Mental Conflict and Misconduct*, Chap. XIV, and *Individual Delinquent*, pp. 352 ff.
[3] Healy, *Individual Delinquent*, p. 354.

they in all likelihood are operative, and by proceeding accordingly.

This means a program of substitution. If some wholesome outlet for the energy can be found, misconduct will very frequently cease. Phychoanalysts have much to say about the "sublimation" of sex impulses into works of charity, art, philanthropy, religion. But the same is true of all sorts of other impulses that may be causing trouble.

CASE 12

Tim J. was a rough sort of bully who had been so bad in Sunday School that he had to be expelled, and the next Sunday lay in wait with some other roughnecks he had assembled, with stones to throw at the teachers as they came out. His own teacher, a young man who had tried to prevent his expulsion (and Tim knew it), went to visit Tim in his home. He was not very welcome, but he ignored that fact.

In the home he found squalour and poverty, so that it was no wonder the boys had few high ideals. But he also found one of the boy's interests; it was in a sparrow he had made into a pet. From this he won Tim's interest in other bird lore, and through that into better associations, and finally back into the Sunday School, where the energy formerly expended in making mischief was now used in promoting class morals.

Or, take another case; eight boys arrested for shooting craps, breaking windows and creating all kinds of disturbance in a community where they had the reputation of being " the worst gang in Soho," were induced by a Y. M. C. A. secretary to form themselves into a civic club, which, under his direction, set about to clear the neighbourhood of the very type of evils in which they had been leaders. In such ways Juvenile Court and settlement workers have developed a technique in dealing with boy problems that is rich in suggestion for workers in the church. The technique cannot take the place of religion, cannot produce the best results without it. But it is essential if religion is to have effective course in the lives of the kind of boys that give us the most problems.

X

THE ADULT OFFENDER

WHAT shall we do with the mature man who persistently goes wrong? In former times society had an easy answer: Off with his head! Only a few generations ago there were more than a hundred offenses punishable, under English law, with death. Then we decided that was too severe, and substituted imprisonment under varied conditions and for various periods, after which most of those punished were again turned loose among their fellow-men. But now we find that this has not been very successful as a means of reforming them, for too many of them reverted again to crime. As a consequence not only prison methods, but the whole program of the state in dealing with the criminal, are now being recast. We are not certain yet just what we should do nor how we should do it, but of one thing there is no question, we have not been doing it right and we must find some other way.

But if this is true of the state, it is certainly more true of the Church, for the record of her accomplishments in the way of restoring the criminal to upright living is lamentably short. Here and there through some mission or Salvation Army meeting some man of long criminal career is marvelously converted, but how about the multiplied thousands who every year are released from the various penal institutions of America? The simple fact is we have had no program for helping them. We have perhaps assumed that there was a chance they might come under the influence of some of our missions or street meetings, but generally we have done little for them. Worse than that, we have gone along with other folks in actually making it harder for the released prisoner to come back if he really wants to do so. We brand him as an ex-convict, we hesitate to give him a job, we acquiesce in the police practice of arresting him on suspicion whenever there is a new crime in the neighbourhood which the police are expected to fasten on somebody.

Here is one of the large neglected fields of evangelism on the part of the Church, neglected because the traditional type of evangelism has failed to reach these people generally, and we have assumed there was no other way. But with the development of more progressive methods of penology there is coming today a much larger opportunity for co-operation on the part of spiritual agencies. The indications are this will be almost wholly in the form of casework.

Indeed, modern penology is altogether a program of casework, for it undertakes to study and deal with each convicted person on the basis of his own individuality. It does not know any such thing as " the criminal," but only this criminal and that criminal. It undertakes to study each one and on the basis of careful diagnosis to construct a program for his rehabilitation into wholesome, helpful living. His past is considered only in so far as it throws light on what to undertake for his future. Retribution has no part in it, that being left in the hands of Him who said, " Vengeance is mine, I will repay, saith the Lord."

Ordinarily this program consists of two parts; first, a period of incarnation or restraint, which in the case of those found to be mentally abnormal may perhaps be continued indefinitely, but in other cases is desired to be as short as may appear to be compatible with promise of effective restoration; and, second, a prolonged period of parole, with decreasing oversight as readjustment to normal living progresses.

In both of these periods spiritual agencies need to play an important part, but only the second concerns us here, for the reason that during imprisonment this service is best rendered under and largely by the chaplain, who should be a specialist professionally trained for this work. But when the period of parole begins there is the opportunity for the volunteer Christian worker. It is the aim of every progressive prison manager of today to have every man, as he is released, enabled to go to a job, provided for him if necessary, and to go into the fellowship of people of godly lives and spiritual experience who will help him, particularly through those perilous first days of his freedom.

From the two penitentiaries of which the writer is one of the trustees, there go out every month thirty or forty men on parole, the majority of them with an earnest determination to make good. What a great thing it would be if each of them could be assured this kind of help where he goes!

CASE 13

Mark E. is a typical example of the product of the old-type prison policies. Mark never saw his father. His mother placed him in an orphan asylum when he was two and a half years old, since which time he has never seen her. At eight years of age he got his first job, working in a bakery. From that time on he rustled for himself, working at odd jobs and living wherever he could. Arrested first for a minor offense, in which he participated while under the influence of liquor, he was sent to the penitentiary for two years. Following that period he had only a few months' freedom when he was picked up by the police on suspicion of having participated in a robbery of which it now appears he was entirely innocent, and sent to the penitentiary again, for twenty years. That was under the old prison policy of solitary confinement, silence and lock-step. Out of it he came a broken

man in both mind and body. He will carry the
prison pallour to his death and there is a decided
prison psychosis.

After about a year's freedom he came under the
influence of a clergyman, who was able to befriend
him and thereby to win something of his confidence. Only something of confidence, because he
had come out of his long confinement with such a
grudge against society for what he felt had been
an outrageous injustice done to him, that he could
have little confidence in anyone. While in prison
he had also contracted a drug habit, which now had
him pretty much in its power. However, the
clergyman continued to cultivate his friendship and
gradually Mark came to have implicit confidence
in his new-found friend. A position was found for
him as orderly in a hospital in which he did finely
for a time. Then the old drug appetite came back,
he fell before it and again into drink, and lost his
job. When his money was spent he came back to
his clergyman friend, made a clean breast of it
all, and started again in a new job secured this
time by himself. This time he was able to stay
straight for a much longer time, but again he fell
into his old troubles, and again he came back to
his friend.

The case has now been on hand for more than
ten years. Mark still falls occasionally into drink,
and probably never will be sufficiently strong to
meet the stresses of life unhelped, for the prison

psychosis he has suffered will probably be permanent. But Mark injures no one but himself, and most of the time lives a useful and happy life. He is a brand plucked from the burning that will always be a brand but has ceased to burn.

Not all cases of former convicts who receive help from good people work out well. Indeed, there have been so many tragedies resulting from misguided sympathy for men still criminal at heart, that the greatest caution must constantly be urged, particularly against the convict who comes of his own initiative seeking for help. In very many such cases he is dishonest and has criminal designs. Ordinarily such cases should be undertaken only on recommendation of the prison officers and after full conference with them. Some criminals specialize in mock professions of emotional conversion as a means of carrying on their evil purposes. A noted thief of a generation ago known as " Lop-eared Pete " was such a master at this that he in one case worked himself so far into the good graces of a pastor that he was taken into the pastor's own home. He rewarded the pastor by deceiving his wife, getting her away from home and placing her in a house of ill fame. Later he specialized in making addresses to women's clubs as a reformed criminal, and then using the information he secured among them to rob their houses at night. This is not to say that nothing is to be done for such characters. Something should be done, but it must be left to the skilled hands of professional workers. However, characters of this kind constitute only a minor part of those released from prison. Most of those going out are worthy of trust, if the counsel of the prison officials is followed.

CASE 14

Calvin J. was a typical spoiled city boy, large of his age, of a bullying type, easily becoming a leader in juvenile crime. Indulged by his mother and doubly petted and humoured by his grandmother, who lived with the family and constantly showed that he was her favourite grandchild, he always had his own way, became thoroughly self-willed, was always excused and defended in his wrongdoings. The grandmother had a few hundred dollars in her own right, on which she drew to employ an attorney every time he got into trouble, so that he would not be sent to reform school. At fifteen he was six feet tall, weighed 162 pounds, but was only in the seventh grade of the public school.

Calvin became a thief when still a small boy. When fifteen he was brought the second time into Juvenile Court and placed on probation. As usual, his mother and grandmother made excuses for him, and that in his presence; it was the other boys' fault, there was something wrong with his mind, the usual excuses offered in such cases. While on probation he continued his thefts despite the best efforts of his sponsor, increasing in the boldness and frequency of them, carrying a gun and becoming more and more of the professional type.

A year later he was again convicted of theft, this time getting off on plaint of affected eyesight, despite protest of his sponsor that he should now be sent to a reform school where there could be a careful course of training in habit formation. A year later he was the leader in a series of house robberies in which thousands of dollars' worth of jewelry was taken. For this he was sentenced to a minimum of sixteen years in the penitentiary. This term was later reduced to a minimum of four years.

During his life up to this time he had rarely attended Sunday School or church, though he managed to go enough to be able to tell the judges when arrested that his name was on the Sunday School roll. His people lived in a respectable community, but his religious training was thoroughly neglected.

The sponsor to whom he had been committed three years before his entrance to our penitentiary, continued his interest in Calvin. The correspondence shows that this interest and help constantly grew on the boy's confidence, and was more and more appreciated. For the first time in his life his will was being curbed, and effectually so. Prison discipline, under which he was frequently punished for offenses, usually of wilfulness, stung him deeply. Under it he came to realize how unappreciative he had been of his true friends in former years, and to express a desire to live a better life. His sponsor, a deeply religious man, used every opportunity for skilfully impressing on him that God only could enable him to live the kind of a life he professed to be determined to follow when released. At the end of his minimum of four years he was released on parole under care of the same sponsor.

Calvin returned at once to his old community, got a job, settled down to work and unquestionably set himself to make good and redeem his past. Shortly after this he married a young woman of good family, who, however, knew all about his record. Then came one of those trying experiences which have sent many a former convict into despair; there was a bank robbery in the neighbourhood, the police undertook to fasten it on Calvin, arrested him, put his picture in the local papers and engaged in the familiar boasting of their shrewd work.

The sponsor went to the jail, found Calvin's wife there with him, both of them in tears. Prompt investigation by the sponsor proved beyond question that Calvin was in no sense connected with the robbery, and the police were compelled to release him. It was only one more case where the police felt they had to " get some one," and tried to fasten the crime on an available ex-convict. Fortunately for Calvin, he had a capable sponsor to help him. But he and his wife were compelled to undergo the strain of this renewed and humiliating publicity.

Five years have since passed, and Calvin is still doing finely. The experience with the police cost him the loss of the good job he then had, but another was secured for him, at which he is doing well. He and his wife are living happily, constantly growing in the respect and esteem of those who know them. He probably will never be an outstanding success financially or otherwise. He is a type of character that will always be in need of the strengthening support of others.

But in his church, where the higher ideals are kept before him and he is thrown into fellowship of upright and godly people, with the support of a good wife and that of his sponsor, who still keeps the personal contact, Calvin is a good citizen, an asset to the very community to which he had formerly been a menace. Twelve years now, the sponsor has been on this one case, and he is still at it. But it has been worth while.

CASE 15

Leon S. was a young man of good parentage, his people being of old American stock and members of a Protestant church. His mother died when he was six years old. His father was a good man but severe and in no way companionable to the boy. While he was still in his teens the boy became in-

volved in too great intimacy with a sweetheart, as
a result of which, when her delicate condition was
discovered, he fled to an eastern metropolis. He
seems to have been led to flee by a sense of guilt
and disgrace which he would gladly have communi-
cated to his father had the relations been more
comradely. In the eastern city he secured work,
but in his loneliness and anxiety he made friends
with a man twice his age who already had a prison
record. Within a year he was accused of complic-
ity in a hold-up. He claims that he was not guilty
of this particular crime, but on circumstantial evidence and because of his associations with one who
had " done time," he was pronounced guilty and
sent to the penitentiary, where he served three
years.

During his imprisonment friends interested in his
case a minister who had become pastor of one of
the churches in his home community, and after
another year or so the young man was paroled in
care of his minister friend, though with the peculiar
stipulation that he should go to some other part of
the country for at least a year. He was, however,
given permission to visit his old home, which he
did—and immediately married the young woman
of his former associations, and acknowledged pa-
ternity of her child, now three years old. He then
went on his year's exile, after which he returned
and secured employment with a local corporation.
After two months he was dropped, with the state-

ment that the company did not employ men with
prison records.

At this critical point the support of his minister-
sponsor enabled him to keep from again going to
pieces, and he was finally able to secure a position
in a shop known for its monotonous work and
small pay. He remained there for three months,
and then got on outdoor job paying more and
offering opportunity for advancement. He has
now occupied this position for three years.

When Leon came out of prison his face was
gloomy, he never smiled, his doctor found a depressed heart and low blood pressure. While in
prison, he says, once an appeal made by an earnest
speaker in the chapel service so " got under his
skin " that he bowed, and prayed a covenant
prayer: " O God, if You ever get me out of this
place, I promise You I'll shoot square! "

He set out from prison to fulfil his vow, encouraged by the cheering fellowship of his minister-
sponsor, but still with spirits depressed by the
constant sense of his position. A half-year after
his return from the year's exile, in the midst of the
Christmastide emphasis on peace, good will among
men, the minister-sponsor made his appeal to Leon
to devote his life absolutely to God. There had
been careful seed-sowing, time for mentation, both
conscious and unconscious. Leon was urged to
make his great decision giving God full chance in
his life. He deliberated carefully, made the de-

cision, joined a preparatory class in church membership, which he attended diligently, with studious and thoughtful attention, and began to offer prayers personal and childlike.

From that time his whole life was notably changed. He became cheerful, his voice gained a new inflection, his eyes a new sparkle. He is now a fine-looking, upstanding fellow with square jaw, good profile, clear, deep-set eyes, his voice even, his manner controlled. The old dejected, hunted disheartened manner is gone; he smiles easily, with twinkling eyes.

Three years have now intervened since this change in his life. A second child has come into the little home. The household is neatly and well maintained, and Leon is greatly helped by the love of his devoted wife—who clung to him through all his troubles, manages the household economically and trains the children with good sense and devotion. Leon himself is active in the church, where he is leader of the Boy Scouts and respected and esteemed by all.

Case 16

Bill R. had been an athlete in early life, a professional football player and wrestler. Then he had undertaken to wrestle with John Barleycorn, and was thrown so often and so badly that he was in a padded cell again and again. He became a professional gambler, a political gangster of the worst type and pretty much of a common bum. His wife had left him and was trying as best she could to make a living for herself and two children. Bill managed to pick himself up somewhat, got his family again together and was working at his trade as a boiler-maker, but was still making little progress, when he formed the acquaintance of a Christian worker who took a special interest in him.

Nothing particular was said about religion between them for more than a year, during which time the worker was cultivating Bill's confidence and finding points of common interest, particularly in certain athletic affairs. Then came an opportune time when Bill himself broached the subject of religion and agreed to go to church with his friend. Following the second service which they attended together, they had a frank talk, and Bill decided to give his life to Christ. It was a hard battle Bill had to fight, but he and his friend kept close to each other and every effort was made to enable him to find new and helpful interests in connection with the church.

Sometimes Bill fell short. Two years after his profession of faith, a rather talkative woman in the church remonstrated with his friend that she believed Bill had been drinking again. " I know far more about that," said his friend, " than you do, but I'm keeping my mouth shut, and I hope you will do the same. Bill is fighting an awful battle, and we must help him."

Two years more passed; Bill had been doing finely. Then came his severest test. His only son, a promising young man of twenty in whom Bill's heart was pretty much wrapped up, sickened and suddenly died. At his death bed his friend had closed the eyes of the young man, then turned to Bill. Reaching out his great hand, Bill said, " God only knows what this means to me. My life was wrapped up in that boy. But God has made no mistake. In this loss I think I hear His call to give my life to helping other fellows who are down and out as I have been! "

Nearly twenty years have since elapsed, and Bill still keeps on, true to his vow and greatly used of God in the service to which he devoted himself beside the dead body of his beloved son.

XI

THE DEFECTIVE HOME

THE family is the mainstay of civilization, the basic structure in our social order. But at the same time it is the most frequent source of the social and religious workers' problems. Domestic discord and unsavoury home conditions are the constant causes of all sorts of other troubles and misdoings. A careful study of some three thousand boy cases figuring in the Morals Court of one of our cities showed that over 80 per cent of them were family problems. That is, the home went wrong, and as a result the boy went wrong. Some of them were just broken homes; father or mother dead and perhaps a step-parent who could not get along with the boy. Many were divorce cases where friction and turmoil had resulted in separation and the boy more or less adrift. Still more were homes full of discord, perhaps a drunken father or querulous, scolding or gad-about mother. Poverty, filth, immorality, many were the features found, but ordinarily in some breakdown of wholesome family relations was found the cause of the boy's going astray.

Similar studies have shown much the same to be true of girls who have gone wrong. It is significant that 21 per cent of the over five hundred prostitutes whose life stories were referred to in an earlier chapter, had come directly from their homes and never worked for wages. Many of Healy's girl cases show home conditions as the cause of wrong-doing. Undue suppression of normal desires for amusement or the company of other young people, overwork with imposition of drudgeries that should not be placed on young shoulders, overcrowding with consequent indecencies and loss of modesty, untidiness and unattractiveness of the home itself, scoldings and naggings and multiform petty cruelties, in things like these the experienced case worker learns to look first for the causes of girls going astray.

Here also are found very common causes of mental cases of the milder sort, particularly suppressions and resultant complexes. Mary L. was a real problem. A girl of only fourteen, she was already sexually immoral, a confirmed runaway who would sleep out under the sidewalks or in old sheds, becoming unspeakably filthy, careless, reckless, retarded in school, in which she had only reached the fourth grade. It took the skilled worker in charge many months to find the cause. Mary was a bit tongue-tied, nervous, and as a result easily confused so that she could not do her best. A younger sister was exceptionally bright and was always being petted and put forward by the other members of the family, who were in the habit of twitting Mary with her inferiority. The result was an overwhelming inferiority complex that drove Mary into all her misdoings. When this was adjusted the restoration of Mary was rapid and complete.

Whether one should pity the drunkard's wife or the drunkard himself is uncertain till one knows whether it was her wrongdoings that drove him to drink. James L. was notorious for sometimes getting drunk and leaving home. His wife had much to say about his delinquencies and was the recipient of much sympathy till the fact came out that his drunks came only after violent tantrums on her part, in which she had made the home a hell for him, perhaps for days, from which he had fled for refuge in drink. Stella J. had her husband arrested and brought into Morals Court on complaint that he stayed away from home at night and did not properly support her. But when she appeared at court, she was dressed in the latest modish patterns, evidence produced showed he was giving her the greatest part of his income; and she indulged right there in court in a tirade of temper that showed plainly why he so frequently chose to stay away at night.

Most domestic troubles are the result of husband and wife not being adapted to each other. They may both be good people, but evidently they are not good for each other. Their ideals are different, their interests, likes and dislikes, they may be physically unadapted, they perhaps get on each others nerves. Perhaps they should never have been married. But they are, and the question is what shall be done about it all. It will not do to shunt it all aside as not important, for it is important. It is tragic, terribly so. Only those who have experienced it first hand can appreciate its woes. " He jeers at scars who never felt a wound." People who understand have all sympathy and patience as they try to help.

Manifestly there are only two ways out, and some way out is imperative, for certainly God never intended two people to live together in discord. One is separation, divorce, the other is adjustment. The former seems sometimes to be necessary, but society properly demands that it be resorted to only when all else has failed. Particularly is divorce undesirable if there are children involved. But just as much is the presence of children a pressing reason for the discord and turmoil to be escaped; they are so damning to their tender souls. All of which calls for efforts as heroic as may be necessary to secure adjustment. Now, the making of adjustments is the essence of social service. Indeed, as social workers see it, most of life's problems are problems of adjustments. A recent writer entitles his volume devoted to the problems of girls who have gone wrong, *The Uuadjusted*

Girl.[1] Every happy home is the product of more or
less adjustment.   Fortunate is the one where little
is necessary.   But more or less, adjustment is the
only way to happiness, helpfulness and peace.

All of which suggests the importance of religion
in the program of service.   For adjustment can
only come as the result of understanding, to which
is added self-sacrifice, patience, forbearance, self-
control, each seeking first not his own, but
another's good—all of which are the Christian
graces that fruit from fellowship with God revealed
in Jesus Christ as typified by the Master Himself
in the figure of the vine and its branches.   " Religion, as the old marriage ceremony put it, will
sustain and sweeten your marriage relationship as
nothing else can."   Herein lies the occasion for
strongly insisting that Christian workers as such
be enlisted in family casework.   They have to offer
a spiritual dynamic, an access to an invigorating
moral power which is the one thing most wanting
in those types of social service in which religion is
not included.

While most of the factors that go into the
making of family problems are pretty much always
the same, there are three which are distinctive of
present-day life in America, and which figure
rather prominently in the cases with which workers
now have to deal.   The first of these is the fact
that so much more of the life of children and young

---

[1] Wm. I. Thomas.

people is now taken out of the home. From day
nursery and kindergarten through school years in
which more and more of the time of the child is
absorbed, and into employment of both young men
and women away from home instead of along with
father and mother as in former times, the oversight and personal influence of both parents and
other members of the family is much less than it
used to be. It is folly to decry this condition. It
is a state that is here to stay, and our task is to
adjust ourselves to it.

The second is the emancipation of women. Of
this her political enfranchisement is only a phase.
Woman today is supposed to be accorded and is
demanding equality in freedom and right to self-
expression with man. Out of this rises not a little
of the domestic discord of modern times. Our
grandfathers were differently situated, for English
law had not yet got entirely away from the thought
of woman as a chattel, and grandfather's wife had
been gravely admonished of her duty to obey.
Family troubles could easily be settled by grandfather asserting his authority and his wife meekly
submitting, for did not the Scriptures declare, " He
shall rule over thee? " Now, this old idea of the
right of the father to even tyrannous mastery over
his household still obtains generally in many of
the countries from which our foreign-born neighbours come, and they bring the idea with them.
This is one of the outstanding difficulties these

people find in making their adjustments to American life.

A third factor, which obtains only among the foreigners, is the abnormal position of the American-born and schooled child in their homes. This child considers itself an American and therefore superior to the parents, who are just ignorant foreigners, unable, perhaps, to speak the language of America and thoroughly unlearned in the American ideals and outlook which the child has picked up among playmates, many of them probably low and perverted. More important still, the parents share the outlook of their children and look up to their children as being really superior to themselves. The effect of all this on parental control is, of course, manifest. All three of these conditions are perhaps passing ones that will later disappear. But while they are here they are potent factors with which we must deal. Examples of all these are to be seen in the family cases already presented in the chapter on " The Foreigner."

CASE 17

Henry R. and his wife had been living a sort of cat-and-dog life for years. Both of them had been reared in foreigners' homes where drinking was common and the ideals anything but high. Henry was a skilled mechanic and worked in a shop where the favourite topics of conversation were drinking bouts, gambling fests and escapades with women.

As long as the saloon remained they both patronized it somewhat, and beer was regularly supplied to the home. After prohibition came, Henry undertook to make "hooch" in his cellar, some of which he sold to his cronies and more of which they drank together on the premises. There were three sons, the youngest now fourteen, the older two about full grown and now starting like their father in dissipation.

Conditions finally became so bad that Mrs. R. found herself rebelling against it all. She had a favourite sister, who likewise was married and had a larger family, but they were all earnest Christian people active in their church. The difference between the two homes so weighed on the mind of Mrs. R., and the increasing abuses on the part of her husband became so great, she felt it all unendurable. She determined to live a different life herself, and tried to get her husband to do the same, but it resulted only in greater abuse on his part.

At last she had him arrested and the case was brought into Morals Court. Henry was highly incensed, and threatened what he would do as soon as some of his shoe-string politician friends from his clubs and hang-outs got busy and had him released. But there were strong social agencies helping his wife and his political friends found themselves powerless. It was thought good for Henry for him just to stay a little while behind the bars till he should get over some of his arrogance and temper, so he was kept in jail a few days. When he seemed somewhat humbled the case was brought into Domestic Relations Court, where after a full hearing Henry was soundly admonished by the court and placed on parole for a year.

During the year he was required to report monthly and each month found himself confronted by an accurate record of how he had been acting. He conducted himself sufficiently well to keep from being put again in jail, but chafed constantly, more so as the year neared its end. When he was finally released from parole he began to carry out some of the threats he had been making of what he would do when the opportunity came. His wife then immediately left him, going into retirement for a week or so in a place provided by some friends. Henry was unable to find her, and went to the social worker who had been his wife's counsellor. Here he was frankly told that his wife would not return as long as he continued to act as he was doing. That she had been doing her best to set things right, but he had not co-operated and the fault was now entirely his.

Henry went home to think it over. The months of his probation had cleared his brain of liquor and set going mental processes of which he was himself hardly conscious. Now it came to fruition. In other words, there had been a subconscious mentation going on which now broke out in a pronounced conversion. Henry convinced the worker of the sincerity of his decision, and the worker then went to work on his wife. She has to be carefully admonished also, particularly not to be hard on her now repentant husband. She returned to the home, there was a gracious reconciliation, the following Sunday, Henry insisted on the whole family going with him to the Methodist church, which they all joined.

And now, after some five years, they are still in the church, living clean and happy Christian lives. It took extreme measures in Henry's case, but he would be the first today to praise those very measures for his salvation.

CASE 18

The wife of Billy M. came to the office of the church agency for counsel about her husband, who had now again disappeared, leaving her pregnant and alone. Enquiry disclosed that this had occurred three times before. When away, sometimes he would send her money, sometimes not. There had been no quarrels, they loved each other, but he would be carried away thus by a sort of wanderlust in which he was utterly thoughtless of her. One of his trips had taken him to England, where he had lived and worked at his trade, for he was a skilled mechanic, for several months.

It took several weeks for the agency to locate her husband, and several more to lure him back. In the meantime the wife was taken care of, the new baby was born, and employment was obtained for her. Then one day he came back, and a conference with the two of them was secured by the worker in charge, following which there was a long, frank talk between the worker (in this case a minister) and Billy. An attractive, well-kept man of perhaps thirty-five, Billy seemed by no means a hard character. He was induced to talk very frankly about relations between himself and his wife, and in that way it was learned there were certain very intimate relationships in which they were not congenial, and which the worker decided were the unconscious but real causes of his disaffections and goings away. These things were then talked over frankly with the wife in his presence, and certain adjustments recommended. Billy was insistent that his wife should give up her employment, he secured a job, and the home was reestablished.

Then followed months of careful watching, in which the worker kept in constant touch with them both. Billy was induced to help in certain lines of social work being carried on by the agency, in which he was quite proficient and in which he found an interest that offset the wanderlust which would still sometimes attack him. His wife also was persuaded to take an interest in the work he was doing and actually participated in it, much to his gratification and pride, for it was in a line in which women are seldom found. Once the wanderlust overcame him, and Billy got away from town. But in a short time he was again in touch with the agency worker and induced to come back.

Twelve years have now elapsed since the case was first taken in charge, and the family is apparently well-established and happy. But the worker never gets entirely out of touch.

Once again it may be asked, what religion had to do with all this? Much all the time. It was as Christian work that the help was given. Counsel always stressed religious resources whenever it was fitting to do so. Much was made of prayer in the counsel given, much of dependence on God in the trying hours. Contact was early formed with the church of their choice, into the Sunday School of which their children were placed and where the whole family still finds its home.

CASE 19

The Spriegers were found living in a little cottage back on an unfrequented alley. There were eight of them at the time, man and wife and six children about as close together in age as possible. Sprieger himself was of old New England stock, but had been thrown on his own resources at ten years of age and rustled about ever since, with little or no religious training. His wife was a saloon keeper's daughter, raised in the saloon, married in the saloon property, where also she had first met her husband. Sprieger was a machinist, a good worker, a good provider for his family. But all of them were without religious ideals or interests; drinking parties and similar sensuous pleasures were their highest concern.

The young minister who discovered them also discovered he was not particularly welcome as a minister, though he was treated with all ordinary courtesy. However, he repeated his call and sent some of the good women of his church to call on Mrs. Sprieger. He soon secured the older children for Sunday School, but aside from this he seemed to be making but little impression. For month after month the program continued, but apparently without results. Ofter he would sit on their porch on pleasant evenings, discussing in a social way various things into which he was able to bring the religious teachings for which he was concerned, but of which they were largely unconscious. For four years this was continued before either the man or his wife entered the church door. But the first day they came, they joined the church.

More than twenty years have followed, during which the whole family have united with the church. Sprieger himself is now senior deacon of the church, his wife is one of the leading and most efficient workers, one son is superintendent of the Sunday School, another is financial secretary of the church, another is in college studying for the Christian ministry. It took four years to make a beginning. But how it paid!

Case 20

One morning, very early, Mrs. Stella White came to the court office in great distress to enter a complaint against her husband, whom she accused of drinking excessively and abusing her. She said that they had been married a number of years, and during his sober intervals he was very kind to her, but she had endured his ill-treatment as long as she could, and had come to the court worker as a last resort. She hoped that the worker would talk with Mr. White in order to influence his future conduct. If this did not bring the desired results, she suggested an arrest. The worker explained to her that the latter remedy was not always the wisest plan, for many times such action only antagonized a man. The worker advised that he be invited to come to the office of his own free will to talk over the matter.

This arrangement was made, and a few days later the couple came in together. The interview resulted in his promising to try to stop drinking and do better. Mr. White said he cared for his wife and wished to keep his home. He blamed his childhood training for his delinquency. When he was a little fellow his mother spoiled him by letting him have his way.

Following this interview, there were many pleasant, as well as unpleasant, visits to the home. The situation remained more or less unchanged for some time, because the husband seemed unable to overcome the drink habit. The worker was successful, however, in interesting the wife in other things, among which was the Bible, a copy of which she gave her. Mrs. White read it every day, and always delighted in discussing Bible stories and asking questions concerning the life of Christ when the worker called.

In a rather personal chat one day, the woman said that she had never thought it possible to have such a valuable friend as the worker, and with tears in her eyes she said that her life would have been different if she had known years before that there were such people as the worker to whom she could have appealed. Then she related something of her life's story.

She had been left an orphan, homeless and friendless just at the age when she most needed guidance and kindly care. She made her way the best she could, never dreaming that there were kind, friendly people in the world. In order to have a home she married a man who drank, gambled and abused her shamefully. Finally, having deserted him, she escaped from one misfortune after another until she became ill and unable to support herself. Then, to avoid becoming dependent upon charity, she married her present husband, who fully understood her marital status. She hoped to legalize this marriage by obtaining a divorce from her first husband, but Mr. White was contented with things as they were.

Mrs. White has a keen intellect and, though not educated, she is refined and appreciates culture. Her appearance indicates sincerity and earnestness. She deplored her past life, which had been distasteful to her, and she endured the situation in which she found herself only because she was helpless and did not know how to change it.

The climax of this story occurred one day when Mrs. White suddenly announced that she had left her husband, and did not intend to go back. She expected to work and take care of herself. For a few days, while work and a home were being found, she lived in the worker's home. In the meantime an attorney was consulted regarding the correct procedure for obtaining a divorce from her first husband.

Mr. White then came forward in a very repentant manner, promised to pay for the divorce, and do anything to make their home a happy one if only she would return to him.

The decree has been granted, and the couple are now very happily situated in their own home, nicely furnished, and almost paid for. They also have a car.

Not so very long ago they visited the worker at her home. Other members of the worker's family liked Mrs. White. The worker and her family were pleased to see how she had improved and were glad to know that Mr. White had not used intoxicating liquor for almost one year. When some one exclaimed: " Why, Stella! You look like a different person, so happy and well! " she replied: " I do not worry now, for I have learned to cast my troubles on the Lord."

Case 21

The Best family came from the mountains of Kentucky, where Best himself had been crippled in a coal mine so that he was permanently incapacitated for work. They were typical mountaineers, slow in speech and action, simple-minded, utterly uninitiated in the ways of city life. They came to a densely crowded industrial town and set up in the midst of a foreign population with the idea that Mrs. Best and the older children would secure employment. The rest of the family consisted of a seventeen-year-old niece; a daughter, eighteen; a son, fourteen; and five younger children. The mother secured employment in a laundry, but her wages barely paid the rent. The others had not secured employment, and the whole family were soon in want.

To make matters worse, the niece and older girl were induced by a couple of young Italian men whom they had met in the community, to take an auto ride, with results disastrous to them; and then found themselves arrested and sentenced to thirty days in jail. Their seducers, after the way of many city police courts, were allowed to go free. This was the stage at which the family was thrown on a Christian agency for help.

This case is still on hand at this writing, and is purposely given here as an example of the need of careful diagnosis and of the way individual cases reveal family problems. It is evident that the cases of these two girls cannot be successfully handled apart from the family itself. It is evident also that the problem here is outstandingly one of adjustment, for these unfortunate mountaineers are certain to be prey in this way of designing persons for a long time, unless given careful oversight. It is not at all improbable that we have here some mental cases also. Economic factors are also at the fore. Of course, most of all are the spiritual needs, but manifestly they cannot be met alone. It is a ministry to the whole of life and that alone that can meet the needs of this case.

Cases like this the traditional evangelism commonly fails to touch. That is because they are cases calling for careful diagnosis, for prolonged treatment, for ministry to the whole of life, for concern for the whole group, for help in making adjustments, and that all in a spirit of Christian service. But this is Casework Evangelism.

PART III

CASEWORK EVANGELISM AND THE CHURCH

XII

PARISH ORGANIZATION

IT will not be many years until the average large church will consider itself as ill equipped for its task without an organized system of case-work as it would today without a Sunday School. This cannot but come in the further development of the courses on which the churches entered years ago. In Shakespeare's time the pastor was pretty much all there was of working staff in the average church. Indeed, he was practically the one person of standing in the community (hence the term " parson," a corruption of " person "), for often he was the only one of education, and so he was the one counsellor and guide of his people in almost everything from writing their wills and drawing their contracts to teaching their children, super-vising their charity and shriving their souls. The differentiation of the work of the church has been a development of relatively recent years. The Sunday School itself had only begun at the open-ing of the last century and the century was half over before it got well under way. Young peo-ple's organizations, like the Christian Endeavour Society, came near its close, as did many of the other agencies most in evidence in the modern church.

Today the whole trend is in the direction of staff organization. Fewer churches and larger is the order of the day. Instead of the familiar small church of our fathers' time with one poorly paid pastor trying to be a man-of-all-work about it, we are working toward large churches, each headed by a pastor who specializes in his distinctive tasks, and has associated with him specialists in religious education, young people's and children's work and such other programs as the parish appears to need. This is in line with the whole trend of modern life and in every way makes for efficiency and economy.

Now, aside from the worship itself, which will always be under the immediate direction of the pastor, there are two major responsibilities in the work of the local church; they are religious education and personal service. Evangelism is not to be thought of as something alongside of these in a separate department, but as something with which they should all be shot through and through. For religious education we have in recent years developed a quite clearly defined program, with an ideal in which there is a director of religious education at the head, who is an employed expert trained for his task, and with an extensive organization making use of a large number of volunteer workers selected and trained for their special tasks by this director. We also frequently have an employed clerical force for office detail work and employed leadership in music.

But personal service has generally been unorganized. We have left it largely to the pastor, or perhaps given him an " assistant " to relieve him of it as a sort of bothersome drudgery. We have also used it somewhat in our educational and other organizations where we looked on it largely as a means to an end; social calls or sick visits to the members of Bible classes as a means to get them back to the class, and all that sort of thing. We have failed to envision it as one of the great ways in which the Christ life is to be lived and we have failed to organize to that end.

Here is going to be the next outstanding development in the program of organized Christianity. The church of tomorrow will have a department of personal service, headed by a trained expert in casework employed for the task. Under her (for usually we shall employ women), will be as carefully organized a corps of volunteer workers as will grace the Sunday School or any other agency of the church's work. Personal service will be raised to the dignity which rightfully belongs to it, and will be done for its own sake in the spirit of the Master who went about doing good for the sheer joy of doing it. We shall be ashamed that we ever degraded it into a bait to get people to accept our opinions on theological questions or to become additional members for strengthening our favourite society. We shall think of it as something for all the church, just as now we think of religious education as for all the church, but shall also think of it as requiring organized leadership and direction in the same way.

The parish program of casework will include, first of all, a system of education in it; education of the general membership in its nature and values, and of particular workers for carrying out the work of particular types of it. Classes in the psychology and technique of personal service will be among those prized as offering much for widening the horizon, deepening the experience and increasing the usefulness and joy of Christian living. We shall see more of immediate value in knowing the biography of a retarded human soul than the geography of Palestine, more in knowing the keys to mental conflicts that fruit in misconduct than in the keys to some cryptic apocalyptic figure of things that may happen in the last time. We shall not cease to study our Bibles; we shall study them with a new relish as we find therein both inspiration and direction for helping people of our own generation out of their troubles and into wholesome living.

Today, even the average minister knows very little about the technique of casework. The veriest tyro in social service knows more about it than many ministers. Pastors were taught nothing of it in the seminaries. Here is found the real reason social workers object to turning cases over to them; they bungle the cases, neglect them, because not only do they not know how, they do not even know how important are the tasks and how tragic it is that they do not know how. Tomorrow the pastors will have to know enough about casework at least to appreciate its values and to see to it that there is provision made for proper instruction and direction of their people in it, and that there is some one provided under whom the work itself can be intelligently and effectively done.

In the next place, the parish program will include a constant study of the community to locate and diagnose the various cases of need. At present most of the churches minister to those more fortunate types of people in their communities that are able to appreciate and respond to the privileges the churches afford; but tomorrow they will give as much attention and intelligent effort to the help of the others. This will not mean that they will supplant the work of other institutions, such as those for various types of defectives and dependents. On the other hand, they will make more use of these institutions, because the case studies on the part of the church workers will discover the character of need in lives now neglected or misdirected and bring them to these institutions.

Nor will it mean that they will take over the work of charity organizations and similar social agencies; they will make greater use of them than at present. But the Church will feel responsibility for all the people in its parish, for serving them as best it can itself and for enlisting in their help whatever other agencies their cases may require.

Such community studies constantly uncover situations in which the correlation of the work of various agencies is necessary, a correlation the Church can well lead in trying to secure. For example, the lack of facilities for wholesome recreation may be making for juvenile delinquency. The Juvenile Court can struggle with the juvenile delinquent, but the Church is in much better position to agitate for adequate municipal provision of wholesome playground or similar facilities. The police may be conniving in commercialized vice that is enticing young girls into dissolute lives. The rescue home can help the fallen girl, but the Church is in far better position to militate against the hellish traffic. Housing or industrial conditions may be making against wholesome family life, which the Church more effectively than anything else can bring to the attention of those responsible for maintaining or at least permitting them.

This community study will need to be constant. It can never be completed. For new needs, new difficulties will constantly be arising as new people appear and new conditions develop. " The poor ye have with you always." Presumably we will never see the time when there will not be those who will need our helpful service. For that matter, there will probably never be a time when we shall not need the service of one another. It is, perhaps, gratifying in a way to think that one will never be deprived of the joy of serving. But, at any rate, the Church may plan now to do it unceasingly.

Finally, the parish program of the Church will find its consummation in conservation by contacts, in tying up needy lives in helpful relations with those from whom help can be secured. Not all the casework of the parish will be done by the casework director, any more than is that of the Associated Charities by its executive secretary or the work of the Sunday School by its recognized head, but it will generally be done under her direction and not a little of it by her own efforts.

A Y. M. C. A. secretary of wide and successful experience once said: " The best secretary is the one who is not missed when he goes away; he has his committees and the rest of his organization so well trained and functioning together that the work goes right on when he slips away." Something of the same principle obtains here. What the Church needs is not only a skilled worker to do casework for her people, it needs also one able to train and direct her own people in it. Just ordinary people can do casework, but if they try to do it in an ordinary way they fail. They can do it properly when trained and directed by expert hands. Organized charity agencies constantly use volunteer workers in this way, and the Church can do it even better.

No particular form of organization for this work has been shown to be effective to the exclusion of others or is advocated here. In one instance known to the writer, fine effects have been secured with a deaconess assigned to the church by the denominational authorities. When she went onto the field she soon made it evident that she was not there to do the casework for the people of the church, but to lead them in it. With a winsome personality she won them both to herself and to enthusiasm for the work in which she was to lead.

In another case a pastor trained in casework set up a program through the women's organization of his congregation; the women found great joy and manifested real helpfulness. In that case he usually made the contacts himself for the women, made most of the diagnosis and directed the service. What the women did in this way was a recognized part of the regular program of work in their society which they appreciated as of equal importance with, for example, their missionary gifts or educational programs.

When we really get the vision of the kingdom of God as destined to embrace the whole of the life of the people and of our own churches as called and privileged to promote all this in their several areas and of each member of our churches as likewise called and privileged to have a part in it, an organized program of consecrated skilful casework seems natural, inevitable.

XIII

THE MIND OF THE WORKER

THUS far we have been concerning ourselves with the problems of casework that rise from the people we are trying to help. But there are others just as real that have to do with the people undertaking the work, and they should be given just as serious consideration. Failures in casework are ordinarily failures by the case workers. Indeed, they are presumed to be so for the reason that the very nature of casework is such that it is to be presumed it will be continued in one form or another until the solution has been found and the best possible adjustment has been made. It may not be carried through by the same worker, very often it will not, for it is the commonest kind of experience in this field for workers to discover others who can carry on particular tasks with cases they have had in hand better than they can themselves, but it is expected that somehow it will be carried on.

Particularly is this true of casework evangelism, for as Christians we believe that God " is not willing that any should perish," that His " arm is not shortened, that it cannot save," and therefore that we have no choice but to continue our efforts till success is secured.   Here is where the Christian case worker is privileged to have a confidence and an assurance no amount of training and skill in mere social service can ever afford.   We need not be discouraged if results do not come at just the time or the place or even at the hands of the particular worker that we had hoped, for it is not ours to set the times or seasons God has put in His own power, but Christian faith does not doubt that ultimate success will come if only we do our part as we should.   When the work really fails, it is the worker who fails.

And yet this is not to say that only people of extraordinary talents can succeed in this work. On the other hand, a large proportion of those who have been outstandingly successful are people of the most ordinary characteristics generally.   It is not a matter of native talents.   It is one of attitude of mind and soul in regards which are much under one's own control.   It would seem, therefore, that these studies should not be concluded without some suggestions that may be of help in careful and prayerful self-examination on the part of those who are ambitious that they may have part in service of this kind.

First of all is the matter of motives.   We have been having much to say about the motivation and the complexes of the subjects of our study, but how about our own?   For the psychology of motivation

is always pretty much the same. Just as some suppressed impulses and resultant complexes and mental conflict motivate crime and other wrongdoing,
so others move to wholesome and helpful undertakings. All conduct is the product of complicated
mental processes, of which much is subconscious
and as difficult of apprehension as in the case of
the person given to outbreaking misconduct.
What, then, are the motives that lead us into social
service and into casework of the kind we have
been discussing? Is it possible that here is to be
found the explanation of some failures?

The question is by no means an easy one, for if
there is anything psychoanalysis has shown, it is
that our controlling motives are very commonly not
at all the ones we think they are. We are driven
to our courses by powerful factors in our subconscious life of which we are unaware, while we
naïvely assume we have done so for the other and
apparently manifest reasons. You cannot determine why a man does as he does merely from the
reason he gives. And neither can he.

Actually prurient elements may unconsciously
enter. In a Southern city a few years ago there
was a case in which an erring girl had become im-
properly intimate with a married man of good
standing in the community. Another man, an
active church worker knowing them both, undertook to help them out of their wrongdoing, which
he did by counselling with the girl and trying by

gaining her esteem and confidence to lead her to
desist. But in so doing he himself soon became
enmeshed with the girl in a worse way than the
other man had been.

At first his friends were inclined to pass the
usual harsh judgment of " hypocrite," but, knowing
his upright life for so many previous years as they
did, they were not content with this. Instead, one
of them, in kindly counsel with him, went carefully
into a study of how it had all come about. Together they came to realize that his real incentives
to interfere in the case had not been merely or even
chiefly the friendly concern for the good names and
proper conduct of his friends he himself supposed
they were, but a prurient pleasure in contemplating
such things of sex.

It was all very humbling, but it was helpful.
These two men counselled and prayed much together over it all till finally the battle was won, the
illicit relation was broken up by mutual consent
and agreement, and the latest reports indicate that
all those involved are now sincerely and successfully living lives in conformity to approved moral
standards. The same psychology will probably
account for the numerous cases in which persons
active in corrective programs regarding such evils
have themselves later fallen into them.

Apparently at the other extreme, there is evidence that some persons particularly severe in their
condemnations of sins of sex are unconsciously

moved thereto by a complex resultant from sex dis-appointment in their own experience which has soured their dispositions and produced this attitude of intense resentment. The experience has prob-ably been entirely forgotten, may have been largely unconscious at the time, but Freud at least would insist it accounts for the present attitude. Accord-ing to this, Jesus had the same psychology in mind when He challenged the harsh critics of His time: " Let him that is without sin among you first cast a stone." He saw what in their own experiences had made them thus severe. This also should be most humbling to us when we find ourselves in-clined to harsh, impatient judgments of others. Of course, it can only lead to failure in our efforts at service.

Another group of motives against which we need to be constantly guarded is a mere prying or even morbid curiosity. This can easily camouflage it-self into what it considers respectability by calling itself " scientific." But it is mere unholy and un-kind curiosity just the same. Persons who clamour to go " slumming " just that they may observe the miseries of the poor and the follies of the dissolute, need to pray much for the forgiveness of God and the shriving of their souls. If one loves to think and talk about the wrongdoings or shortcomings of those he is supposed to help, and can do so without pangs of sympathetic sorrow, it is an indication that his interest is of this unworthy kind. If one concerns himself with social and spiritual diagnosis and is satisfied with just that; if one enjoys studying humans to determine why they act as they do, and stops with that, he may perhaps be a scientist, but he can never in this way become a successful case worker.

The one fruitful Christian motive is that in which a person seeks to serve, one in which joy is found in seeing other lives helped and in the consciousness that it has been as a result of one's own effort. Under this one seeks to know only that he may the more successfully help, diagnosis is of interest only as a basis for helpful treatment, survey is valued only as a basis for program. It is the spirit of Paul when he found his soul " stirred within him as he saw the city wholly given to idols," and as he cried in the face of a needy, sinful world, " Woe is me if I preach not the gospel! " It is the spirit of our Lord Himself who " for the joy that was set before him "—the joy of beholding a world saved by His loving sacrifice—" endured the cross, despising the shame! " Casework undertaken from motives such as this can never fail.

How much the case worker needs to go apart anon, and say like the Psalmist of old, " Search me, O Lord, and know my heart; try me, and make plain my life purposes! Let me know if there be any unrighteous way in me, and lead me in the way everlasting. Then will I teach transgressors thy way, and sinners shall be converted unto thee."

A second concern that should be on the mind of the worker is the persistent perseverance that "stays through." Much has been said in these discussions about the importance of the time element, the frequency of failure because of impatience. But this is not always easy. It is usually difficult. To go right ahead with full confidence in face of repeated apparent failures and lack of response or even appreciation, to begin all over again when one who had started in better living falls back once more into old misconduct and even worse, all this is not hard to talk about. But it is hard to do. And yet it is essential to success.

There is one and only one thing that can sustain it constantly. That is Christian faith. " Is God dead? " asked Luther's wife when once he was apparently in despair. " Right is right, since God is God, and right the day will win; to doubt would be disloyalty, to falter would be sin," is the Christian assurance. This is, after all, God's world, and God is good. This the Christian profoundly believes. We, in undertakings like these, are " workers together with God," and despite our weaknesses and follies, " beneath us are the everlasting arms." That is the Christian's confidence.

But with all this, and with the renewal of strength of faith and purpose that comes from one's quiet hours alone with God, there still come times when the wearied worker needs something more. Here comes the value of meetings, of the

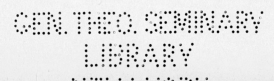

assembling of fellow-Christians for hours or even for days of conference together and prayer together, as well as the regular privileges of worship in the sanctuary. " They that loved the Lord spake often one with another," in New Testament times, and they still need to do so.

Jesus made a practice of gathering His disciples together for instruction and inspiration. When He sent out the Twelve and afterwards the Seventy, it was from meetings in which He had stirred them with enthusiasm; and when they returned He assembled them again.

The values of the old-time protracted meetings were probably more in their being " revivals " than " times of ingathering," and of those values we are still in need. The meetings which are not now so efficacious as formerly for reaching the unsaved are none the less needed and precious for the help of those who are to work outside in a sinful, suffering world. We still need to adhere to the counsel, " Forsake not the assembling of yourselves together."

Printed in the United States of America